STAAR MASTER®
Revised for the Most Recent TEKS

Student Practice Book
Mathematics, Grade 3

for the State of Texas Assessments
of Academic Readiness

Lori Mammen
Editorial Director

ISBN: 978-1-60539-904-1

Copyright infringement is a violation of Federal Law.

©2014, 2015, 2016 by ECS Learning Systems, Inc., Bulverde, Texas. All rights reserved. No part of this publication may be reproduced, translated, stored in a retrieval system, or transmitted in any way or by any means (electronic, mechanical, photocopying, recording, or otherwise) without prior written permission from ECS Learning Systems, Inc.

Reproduction of any part of this publication for an entire school or for a school system, by for-profit institutions and tutoring centers, or for commercial sale is strictly prohibited.

Printed in the United States of America. STAAR MASTER is a registered trademark of ECS Learning Systems, Inc.

Disclaimer Statement

ECS Learning Systems, Inc. recommends that the purchaser/user of this publication preview and use his/her own judgment when selecting lessons and activities. Please assess the appropriateness of the content and activities according to grade level and maturity of your students. The responsibility to adhere to safety standards and best professional practices is the duty of the teachers, students, and/or others who use the content of this publication. ECS Learning Systems is not responsible for any damage, to property or person, that results from the performance of the activities in this publication.

STAAR is a registered trademark of the Texas Education Agency. STAAR MASTER and ECS Learning Systems, Inc. are not affiliated with or sponsored by the Texas Education Agency or the State of Texas.

Table of Contents

Mathematics Chart **4**

Reporting Category 1 .... **5**
Numerical Representations and Relationships

Reporting Category 2 .... **43**
Computations and Algebraic Relationships

Reporting Category 3 .... **97**
Geometry and Measurement

Reporting Category 4 .... **127**
Data Analysis and Personal Financial Literacy

Reference Materials **143**

ECS Learning Systems, Inc.
P. O. Box 440
Bulverde, TX 78163-0440
ecslearningsystems.com
1.800.688.3224 (t)
1.877.688.3226 (f)
customercare@ecslearningsystems.com

Grade 3
Mathematics Chart

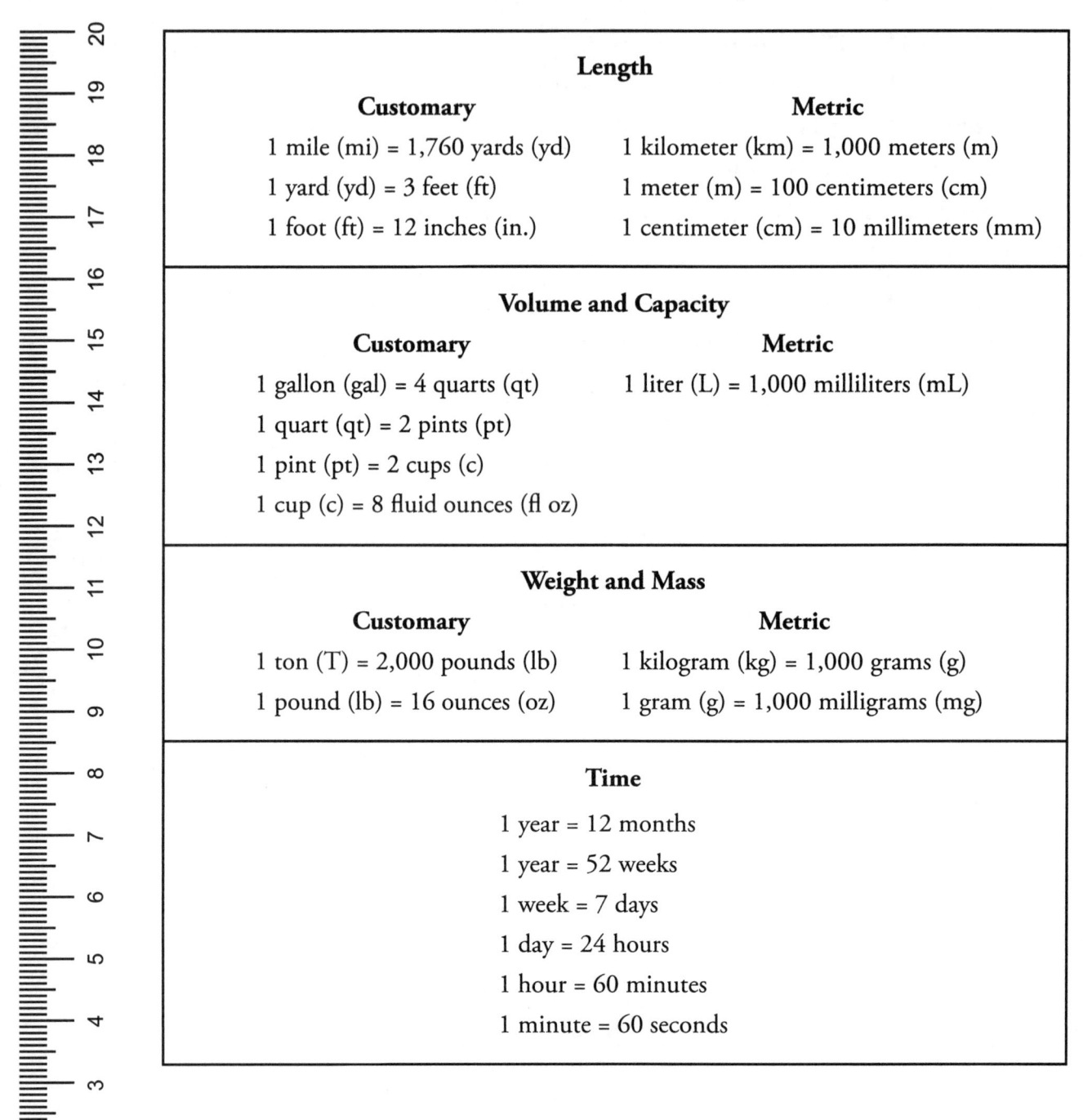

Length

Customary

1 mile (mi) = 1,760 yards (yd)

1 yard (yd) = 3 feet (ft)

1 foot (ft) = 12 inches (in.)

Metric

1 kilometer (km) = 1,000 meters (m)

1 meter (m) = 100 centimeters (cm)

1 centimeter (cm) = 10 millimeters (mm)

Volume and Capacity

Customary

1 gallon (gal) = 4 quarts (qt)

1 quart (qt) = 2 pints (pt)

1 pint (pt) = 2 cups (c)

1 cup (c) = 8 fluid ounces (fl oz)

Metric

1 liter (L) = 1,000 milliliters (mL)

Weight and Mass

Customary

1 ton (T) = 2,000 pounds (lb)

1 pound (lb) = 16 ounces (oz)

Metric

1 kilogram (kg) = 1,000 grams (g)

1 gram (g) = 1,000 milligrams (mg)

Time

1 year = 12 months

1 year = 52 weeks

1 week = 7 days

1 day = 24 hours

1 hour = 60 minutes

1 minute = 60 seconds

Reporting Category 1
Numerical Representations and Relationships

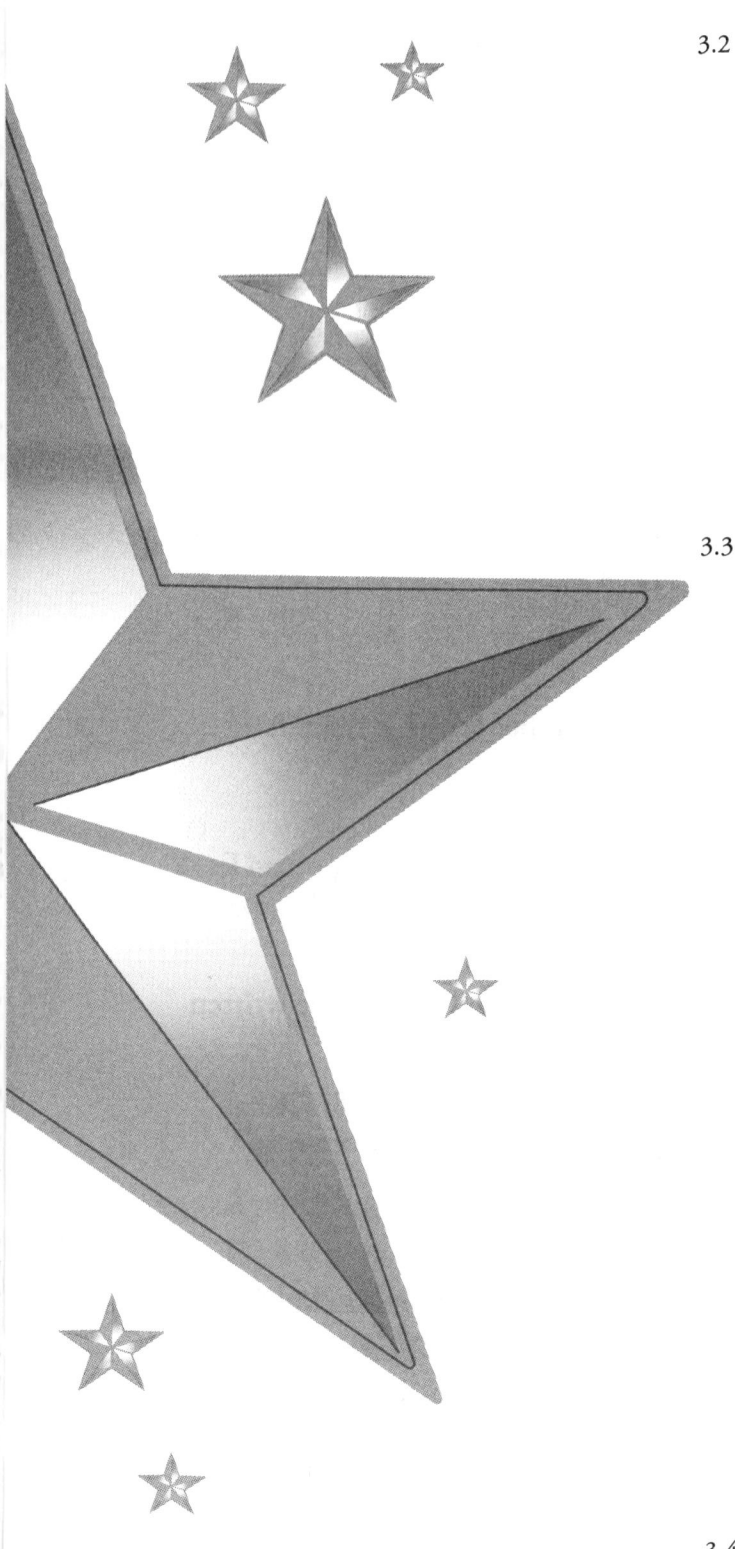

3.2 A. Compose and decompose numbers up to 100,000 as a sum of so many ten thousands, so many thousands, so many hundreds, so many tens, and so many ones using objects, pictorial models, and numbers, including expanded notation as appropriate (Readiness Standard)

B. Describe the mathematical relationships found in the base-ten place value system through the hundred thousands place (Supporting Standard)

C. Represent a number on a number line as being between two consecutive multiples of 10; 100; 1,000; or 10,000, and use words to describe relative sizes of numbers in order to round whole numbers (Supporting Standard)

D. Compare and order whole numbers up to 100,000, and represent comparisons using the symbols >, <, or = (Readiness Standard)

3.3 A. Represent fractions greater than zero and less than or equal to one with denominators of 2, 3, 4, 6, and 8 using concrete objects and pictorial models, including strip diagrams and number lines (Supporting Standard)

B. Determine the corresponding fraction greater than zero and less than or equal to one with denominators of 2, 3, 4, 6, and 8 given a specified point on a number line (Supporting Standard)

C. Explain that the unit fraction 1/*b* represents the quantity formed by one part of a whole that has been partitioned into *b* equal parts where *b* is a non-zero whole number (Supporting Standard)

D. Compose and decompose a fraction *a*/*b* with a numerator greater than zero and less than or equal to *b* as a sum of parts 1/*b* (Supporting Standard)

E. Solve problems involving partitioning an object or a set of objects among two or more recipients using pictorial representations of fractions with denominators of 2, 3, 4, 6, and 8 (Supporting Standard)

F. Represent equivalent fractions with denominators of 2, 3, 4, 6, and 8 using a variety of objects and pictorial models, including number lines (Readiness Standard)

G. Explain that two fractions are equivalent if and only if they are both represented by the same point on a number line or represent the same portion of a same size whole for an area model (Supporting Standard)

H. Compare two fractions having the same numerator or denominator in problems by reasoning about their sizes and justifying the conclusion using symbols, words, objects, and pictorial models (Readiness Standard)

3.4 I. Determine if a number is even or odd using divisibility rules (Supporting Standard)

3.7 A. Represent fractions of halves, fourths, and eighths as distances from zero on a number line (Supporting Standard)

Reporting Category 1
Numerical Representations and Relationships

Exercise 3

3.2A: Compose and decompose numbers up to 100,000 as a sum of so many ten thousands, so many thousands, so many hundreds, so many tens, and so many ones (Readiness Standard)

(3.1F)
1. In which number does the 5 represent 5 × 10,000?

    A 5,103
    B 6,582
    C 105,739
    D 750,839

(3.1D; 3.1F)
2. The model below represents a number.

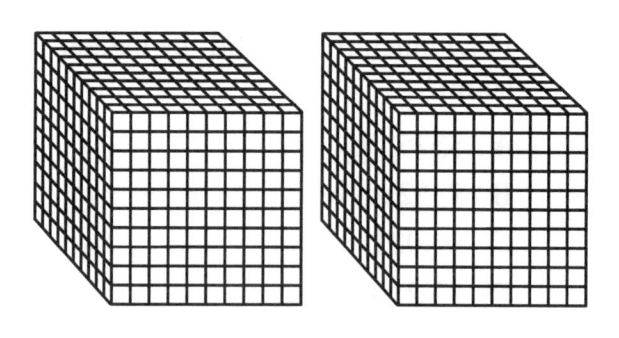

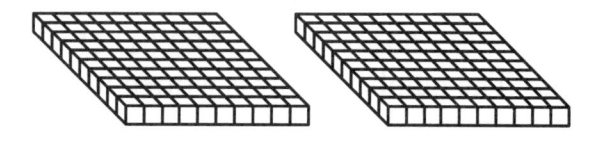

    What number does the model represent?

    A 223
    B 2,023
    C 2,203
    D 2,230

(3.1F)
3. What number belongs in the blank below?

    _____ + 700 + 10 = 1,710

    A 10
    B 100
    C 1,000
    D 10,000

(3.1F)
4. The number below is written in expanded form.

    10,000 + 9,000 + 600 + 1

    How would the number be written in standard form?

    A 1,961
    B 19,601
    C 19,610
    D 109,601

Reporting Category 1
Numerical Representations and Relationships

Exercise 4

3.2A: Compose and decompose numbers up to 100,000 as a sum of so many ten thousands, so many thousands, so many hundreds, so many tens, and so many ones (Readiness Standard)

(3.1F)
1. How is the number 69,108 written in expanded form?

    A 6,000 + 900 + 10 + 8
    B 6,000 + 900 + 100 + 8
    C 60,000 + 900 + 100 + 8
    D 60,000 + 9,000 + 100 + 8

(3.1D; 3.1F)
2. The model below represents a number.

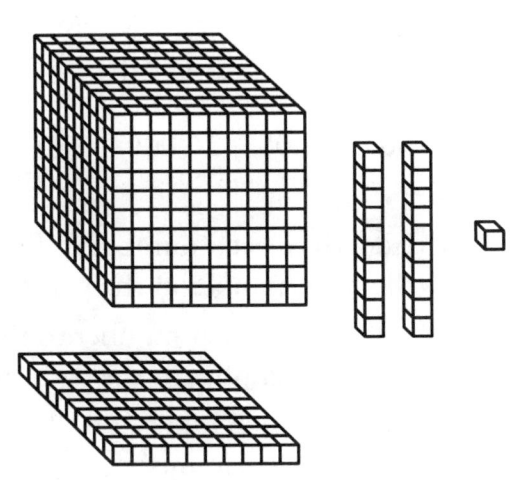

    What number does the model represent?

    A 112
    B 1,112
    C 1,121
    D 11,121

(3.1F)
3. The distance (in kilometers) around Earth at the equator is shown in expanded form below.

    $$40,000 + 70 + 5$$

    What is this distance written in standard form?

    A 475 km
    B 4,075 km
    C 40,075 km
    D 40,750 km

(3.1A; 3.1D; 3.1E)
4. The chart below shows the number of toys a warehouse ships in a box, a case, a carton, and a crate.

Container	Number of Toys
Box	10
Case	100
Carton	1,000
Crate	10,000

    Last week, the warehouse shipped 8 crates, 9 cartons, 4 cases, and 7 boxes of toys. How many toys did the warehouse ship?

    A 28
    B 894
    C 8,947
    D 89,470

Reporting Category 1
Numerical Representations and Relationships

Exercise 5

3.2B: Describe the mathematical relationships found in the base-ten place value system through the hundred thousands place (Supporting Standard)

Use the information below to answer questions 1–3.

Look at the place value chart below.

Millions	Hundred thousands	Ten thousands	Thousands	Hundreds	Tens	Ones
			5			

(3.1E)
1. What number is represented by the 5 in the place value chart?

    A 5
    B 50
    C 500
    D 5,000

(3.1E)
2. What number is 10 times the number written in the place value chart?

    A 500
    B 5,000
    C 50,000
    D 500,000

(3.1E)
3. If you divided the number in the place value chart by 100, in what column would you write the 5?

    A Ones
    B Tens
    C Hundreds
    D Thousands

(3.1C; 3.1F; 3.1G)
4. Which sentence best describes the rule used to find the numbers in the pattern below?

    26   260   2,600   26,000   260,000

    A Add 10 to each number to find the next number in the pattern.
    B Add 100 to each number to find the next number in the pattern.
    C Multiply each number by 10 to find the next number in the pattern.
    D Multiply each number by 100 to find the next number in the pattern.

Reporting Category 1
Numerical Representations and Relationships

Exercise 6

3.2B: Describe the mathematical relationships found in the base-ten place value system through the hundred thousands place (Supporting Standard)

(3.1D; 3.1F)

1. What factor makes the following equation true?

    _____ × 6,870 = 687,000

    A 1
    B 10
    C 100
    D 1,000

(3.1F)

2. Look at the place value chart below.

Millions	Hundred thousands	Ten thousands	Thousands	Hundreds	Tens	Ones
		1	0	0	0	0

    How many tens are in 10,000?

    A 10
    B 100
    C 1,000
    D 10,000

(3.1D; 3.1F)

3. Look at the place value chart below.

Millions	Hundred thousands	Ten thousands	Thousands	Hundreds	Tens	Ones

    In which column would you write the number 6 to show the answer for the equation below?

    1,000 × 16 = _____

    A Hundreds
    B Thousands
    C Ten-thousands
    D Hundred-thousands

(3.1F)

4. One day is 24 hours long. How many hours are in 100 days?

    A 240
    B 2,400
    C 24,000
    D 240,000

Reporting Category 1
Numerical Representations and Relationships

Exercise 7

3.2B: Describe the mathematical relationships found in the base-ten place value system through the hundred thousands place (Supporting Standard)

(3.1D; 3.1F)
1. What number makes the following equation true?

    1,000 × _____ = 13,000

    A 13
    B 103
    C 130
    D 1,300

(3.1D; 3.1F)
2. A student wrote the following number in a place value chart.

    54,832

    If the student multiplied the number by 10, the product would be—

    A 154,832
    B 504,832
    C 540,832
    D 548,320

(3.1D; 3.1F)
3. What number makes the following equation true?

    _____ × 2,450 = 24,500

    A 1
    B 10
    C 100
    D 1,000

(3.1F)
4. Look at the place value chart below.

Millions	Hundred thousands	Ten thousands	Thousands	Hundreds	Tens	Ones
			4			

    If you move the 4 one place to the right, what number does it represent?

    A 4
    B 40
    C 400
    D 40,000

(3.1D; 3.1F)
5. What number makes the following equation true?

    641,000 ÷ 10 = _____

    A 64
    B 641
    C 6,410
    D 64,100

Reporting Category 1
Numerical Representations and Relationships

Exercise 8

3.2C: Represent a number on a number line as being between two consecutive multiples of 10; 100; 1,000; or 10,000, and use words to describe relative size of numbers in order to round whole numbers (Supporting Standard)

(3.1D; 3.1E; 3.1F)
1. Which letter on the number line below marks the point closest to 47?

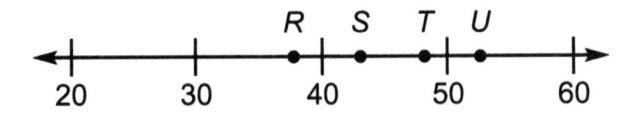

   A Point R
   B Point S
   C Point T
   D Point U

(3.1D; 3.1E; 3.1F)
2. What is the best estimate for the whole number marked by the arrow on the number line below?

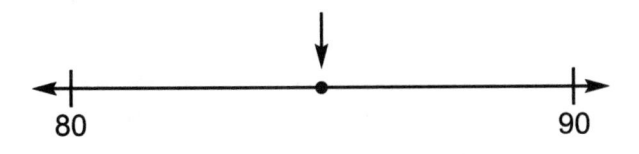

   A 82
   B 83
   C 85
   D 88

(3.1D; 3.1E; 3.1F)
3. On which number line is the letter X closest to the number 9,700?

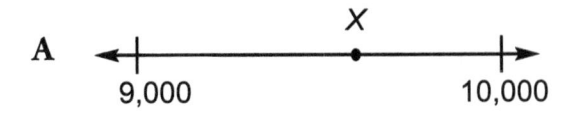

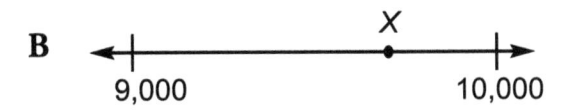

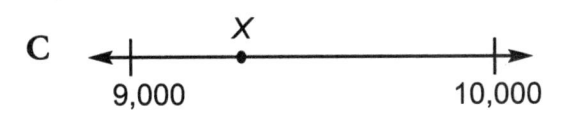

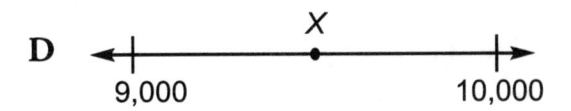

(3.1D; 3.1E; 3.1F)
4. What is the best estimate for the whole number marked by the arrow on the number line below?

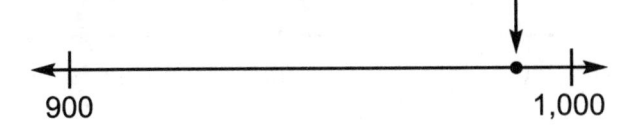

   A 930
   B 940
   C 950
   D 990

© ECS Learning Systems, Inc.

STAAR MASTER® Student Practice Book—Math, Grade 3   13

Reporting Category 1
Numerical Representations and Relationships

Exercise 9

3.2C: Represent a number on a number line as being between two consecutive multiples of 10; 100; 1,000; or 10,000, and use words to describe relative size of numbers in order to round whole numbers (Supporting Standard)

(3.1E; 3.1F)

1. On which number line is the letter *P* closest to the number 520?

   A ← | — P — | →
         500   600

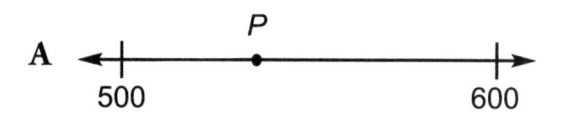

   B ← | ——— P ——— | →
         500   600

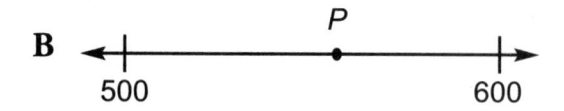

   C ← | ——————— P — | →
         500   600

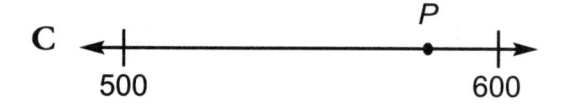

   D ← | — P ——————— | →
         500   600

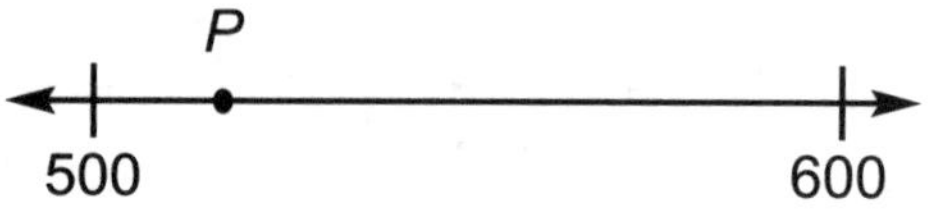

(3.1E; 3.1F)

2. Which letter on the number line below marks the point closest to 98?

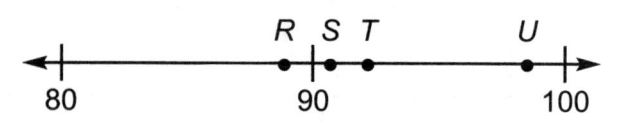

   ← | — R S T — U — | →
     80   90   100

   A Point *R*
   B Point *S*
   C Point *T*
   D Point *U*

(3.1E; 3.1F)

3. What is the best estimate for the whole number marked by the arrow on the number line below?

   ← | — ↓ ——————— | →
     700   800

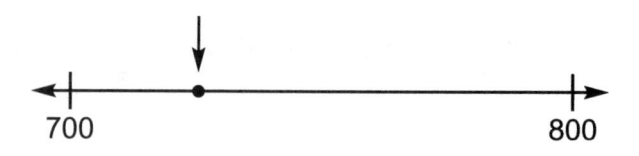

   A 702
   B 710
   C 725
   D 750

(3.1E; 3.1F)

4. What is the best estimate for the whole number marked by the arrow on the number line below?

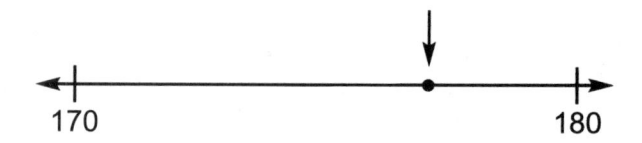

   ← | ——————— ↓ — | →
     170   180

   A 172
   B 175
   C 177
   D 179

Reporting Category 1
Numerical Representations and Relationships

Exercise 10

3.2D: Compare and order whole numbers up to 100,000, and represent comparisons using the symbols >, <, or = (Readiness Standard)

(3.1A; 3.1D; 3.1E; 3.1F)

1. The chart below shows the distance from San Antonio, Texas to four other cities.

Distances Between Cities

City	Distance from San Antonio (in miles)
Buffalo, New York	1,653
Norfolk, Virginia	1,579
Pittsburgh, Pennsylvania	1,505
Washington, D.C.	1,609

Which expression correctly compares the shortest and longest distances listed in the chart?

A 1,505 < 1,579
B 1,609 > 1,505
C 1,653 > 1,505
D 1,653 > 1,609

(3.1F)

2. Which number correctly completes the expression below?

_____ > 5,184

A 5,075
B 5,090
C 5,104
D 5,201

(3.1F)

3. Which number is greater than 80,023 and less than 80,203?

80,023 < _____ < 80,203

A 80,013
B 80,132
C 80,208
D 80,302

(3.1D; 3.1F)

4. What number could be written between 815 and 909 on the number line below?

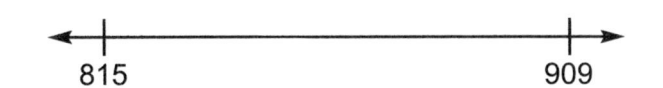

815 ———————————— 909

A 795
B 809
C 864
D 913

(3.1F)

5. Which group shows the numbers in order from least to greatest?

A 24,590 25,509 24,950 25,905
B 24,590 24,950 25,509 25,905
C 25,905 25,509 24,950 24,590
D 25,509 25,905 24,590 24,950

Reporting Category 1
Numerical Representations and Relationships

Exercise 13

3.3A: Represent fractions greater than zero and less than or equal to one with denominators of 2, 3, 4, 6, and 8 using concrete objects and pictorial models (Supporting Standard)

(3.1A; 3.1D; 3.1F)

1. The diagram below represents a hiking trail in a park.

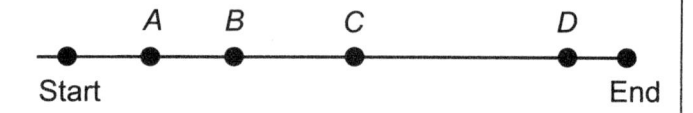

   ```
           A   B       C           D
   •───•───•───•───────•───────────•───•
   Start                              End
   ```

   If a hiker begins at "Start," at which point will the hiker have traveled about $\frac{1}{3}$ of the trail?

   A Point *A*
   B Point *B*
   C Point *C*
   D Point *D*

(3.1D)

2. Look at the box below.

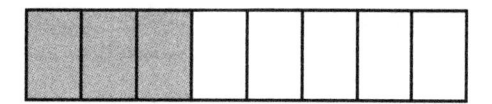

   What fraction of the box is shaded?

   A $\frac{1}{4}$
   B $\frac{1}{3}$
   C $\frac{3}{8}$
   D $\frac{3}{4}$

(3.1D)

3. Which diagram shows $\frac{2}{3}$ of the box shaded?

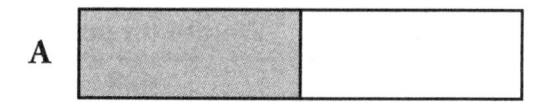

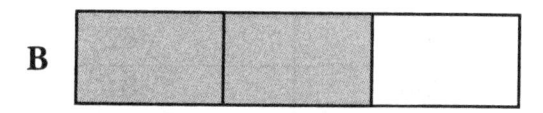

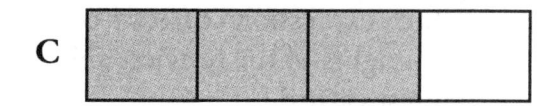

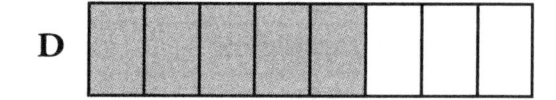

   A
   B
   C
   D

(3.1D)

4. Look at the box below.

   What fraction of the box is shaded?

   A $\frac{1}{6}$
   B $\frac{2}{3}$
   C $\frac{3}{4}$
   D $\frac{5}{6}$

Reporting Category 1
Numerical Representations and Relationships

Exercise 14

3.3A: Represent fractions greater than zero and less than or equal to one with denominators of 2, 3, 4, 6, and 8 using concrete objects and pictorial models (Supporting Standard)

(3.1D)

1. The picture below shows several candy canes.

   What fraction of the candy canes are broken?

   A $\frac{1}{6}$

   B $\frac{2}{6}$

   C $\frac{1}{2}$

   D $\frac{2}{3}$

(3.1D; 3.1F)

2. Look at the number line below.

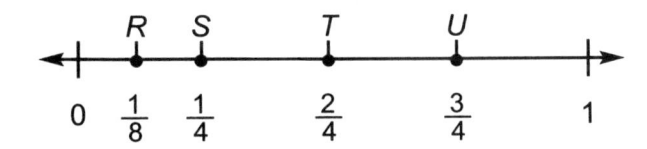

   R S   T   U
   0 $\frac{1}{8}$ $\frac{1}{4}$ $\frac{2}{4}$ $\frac{3}{4}$ 1

   Which point on the number line could also represent $\frac{1}{2}$?

   A Point R
   B Point S
   C Point T
   D Point U

(3.1A; 3.1D)

3. Mia collects stuffed animals. Which drawing shows that $\frac{2}{3}$ of her stuffed animals are rabbits?

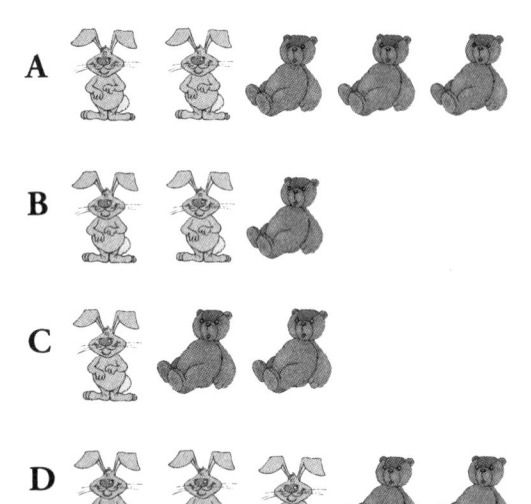

   A
   B
   C
   D

(3.1D)

4. The bracelets below have both white and black beads.

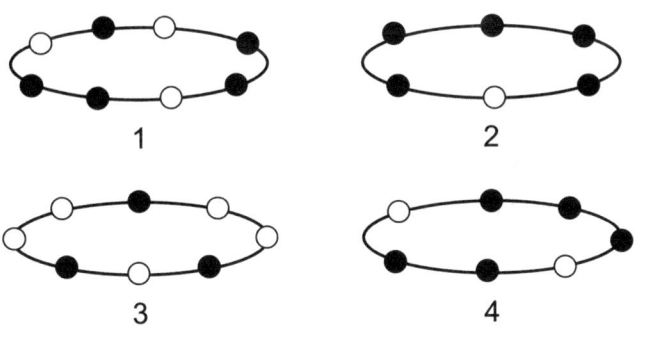

   1   2
   3   4

   On which bracelet are $\frac{5}{8}$ of the beads black?

   A Bracelet 1   C Bracelet 3
   B Bracelet 2   D Bracelet 4

Reporting Category 1
Numerical Representations and Relationships

Exercise 19

3.3D: Compose and decompose a fraction a/b with a numerator greater than zero and less than or equal to b as a sum of parts 1/b (Supporting Standard)

(3.1D; 3.1F)
1. The figure below is partitioned into equal parts.

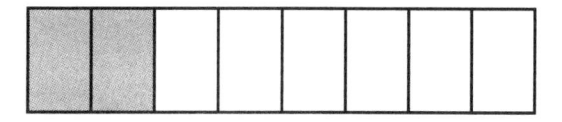

   If 3 more parts are shaded, how much of the figure will be shaded in all?

   A $\frac{1}{8}$

   B $\frac{3}{8}$

   C $\frac{5}{8}$

   D $\frac{6}{8}$

(3.1D; 3.1F)
2. The figures below are partitioned into equal parts.

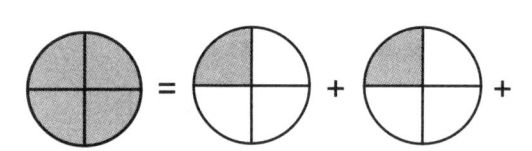

   Which figure belongs in the empty space?

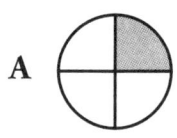

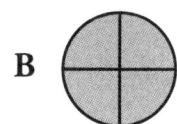

   A   C

   B   D

(3.1F)
3. What fraction correctly completes the equation below?

   $$\frac{3}{6} + \boxed{\frac{}{}} = \frac{6}{6}$$

   A $\frac{1}{6}$

   B $\frac{2}{6}$

   C $\frac{3}{6}$

   D $\frac{4}{6}$

(3.1D; 3.1F)
4. Kyle drew the figure below and partitioned it into equal parts. Then, he shaded some of the parts.

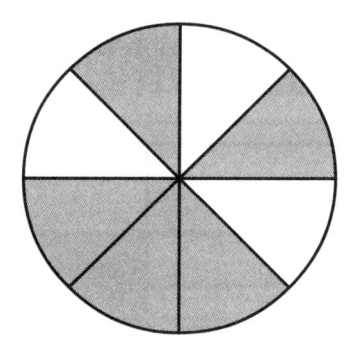

   If Kyle erases the shading from 2 of the shaded parts, what fraction of the figure will still be shaded?

   A $\frac{7}{8}$ C $\frac{5}{8}$

   B $\frac{6}{8}$ D $\frac{3}{8}$

Reporting Category 1
Numerical Representations and Relationships

Exercise 20

3.3D: Compose and decompose a fraction a/b with a numerator greater than zero and less than or equal to b as a sum of parts 1/b (Supporting Standard)

(3.1B; 3.1D; 3.1F)

1. Each of the following expressions shows a correct way to decompose $\frac{5}{6}$ EXCEPT—

   A $\frac{2}{6} + \frac{2}{6} + \frac{1}{6}$

   B $\frac{3}{6} + \frac{2}{6} + \frac{1}{6}$

   C $\frac{1}{6} + \frac{1}{6} + \frac{3}{6}$

   D $\frac{1}{6} + \frac{1}{6} + \frac{1}{6} + \frac{1}{6} + \frac{1}{6}$

(3.1D; 3.1F)

2. Marie drew the figures below and partitioned them into equal parts.

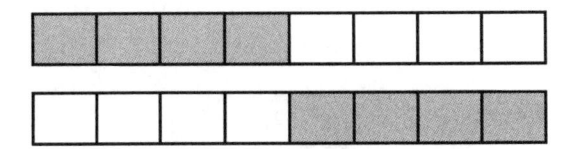

   If she adds the shaded parts of both figures, what fraction of a whole figure will Marie have?

   A $\frac{1}{8}$

   B $\frac{3}{8}$

   C $\frac{7}{8}$

   D $\frac{8}{8}$

Use the following information to answer questions 3 and 4.

Aiden, Jimmy, and Max each bought a bag with 4 pieces of candy.

Aiden   Jimmy   Max

(3.1A; 3.1D; 3.1F)

3. Each boy gave one piece of candy to Jack, another friend. What fraction of the candy remained in each boy's bag?

   A $\frac{3}{4}$ C $\frac{1}{2}$

   B $\frac{2}{3}$ D $\frac{1}{4}$

(3.1A; 3.1B; 3.1F)

4. Which expression shows how much of a bag of candy the boys gave to Jack?

   A $\frac{3}{4} + \frac{3}{4} + \frac{3}{4}$

   B $\frac{1}{2} + \frac{1}{2} + \frac{1}{2}$

   C $\frac{1}{3} + \frac{1}{3} + \frac{1}{3}$

   D $\frac{1}{4} + \frac{1}{4} + \frac{1}{4}$

Reporting Category 1
Numerical Representations and Relationships

Exercise 21

3.3E: Solve problems involving partitioning an object or a set of objects among two or more recipients using pictorial representations of fractions with denominators of 2, 3, 4, 6, and 8 (Supporting Standard)

(3.1A; 3.1D; 3.1F)

1. Clay and Clark shared the orange slices shown below.

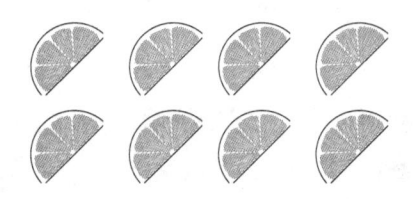

   Clay ate 5 of the slices, and Clark ate 3 of the slices. What fraction of the orange slices did the boys eat?

   A $\frac{2}{8}$ **C** $\frac{5}{8}$

   B $\frac{3}{8}$ **D** $\frac{8}{8}$

(3.1A; 3.1D; 3.1F)

2. Graciela had 6 spaces to fill on a scrapbook page.

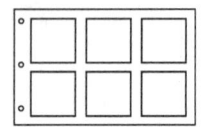

   She filled $\frac{1}{2}$ of the spaces with photographs and left the others empty. Which page could be Graciela's scrapbook page?

   A    **C**

   B 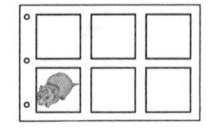   **D**

(3.1A; 3.1D; 3.1F)

3. Mr. Hernandez made the birdhouses shown below.

   He painted 2 birdhouses red, 1 birdhouse green, and 1 birdhouse blue. What fraction of the birdhouses did Mr. Hernandez paint green or blue?

   A $\frac{1}{4}$ **C** $\frac{3}{4}$

   B $\frac{2}{4}$ **D** $\frac{4}{4}$

(3.1A; 3.1D; 3.1F)

4. Jill and Heather ordered the pizza shown below.

   The girls each ate 3 slices of the pizza. What fraction of the pizza did the girls eat?

   A $\frac{2}{8}$ **C** $\frac{2}{3}$

   B $\frac{2}{4}$ **D** $\frac{6}{8}$

Reporting Category 1
Numerical Representations and Relationships

Exercise 22

3.3E: Solve problems involving partitioning an object or a set of objects among two or more recipients using pictorial representations of fractions with denominators of 2, 3, 4, 6, and 8 (Supporting Standard)

(3.1A; 3.1D; 3.1F)

1. Mrs. Morris bought the carton of eggs shown below.

   At home, she found that 2 eggs in the carton were cracked. What fraction of the eggs in the carton were cracked?

   A $\frac{1}{6}$

   B $\frac{2}{6}$

   C $\frac{3}{6}$

   D $\frac{4}{6}$

(3.1A; 3.1D; 3.1F)

2. Tony bought the postage stamps shown below.

   What fraction of Tony's stamps show a picture of an eagle?

   A $\frac{1}{6}$ C $\frac{2}{8}$

   B $\frac{2}{6}$ D $\frac{1}{2}$

(3.1A; 3.1D; 3.1F)

3. Margaret has the coins shown below.

   What fraction of Margaret's coins are quarters?

   A $\frac{1}{8}$

   B $\frac{2}{8}$

   C $\frac{3}{8}$

   D $\frac{4}{8}$

(3.1A; 3.1D; 3.1E)

4. Micah rolled the numbers shown below during a game.

   | 4 | 4 | 5 | 6 |

   What fraction of Micah's numbers were greater than 3?

   A $\frac{1}{4}$

   B $\frac{2}{4}$

   C $\frac{3}{4}$

   D $\frac{4}{4}$

Reporting Category 1
Numerical Representations and Relationships

Exercise 23

3.3F: Represent equivalent fractions with denominators of 2, 3, 4, 6, and 8 using a variety of objects and pictorial models, including number lines (Readiness Standard)

(3.1D; 3.1F)

1. Which point on the number line below represents $\frac{3}{6}$?

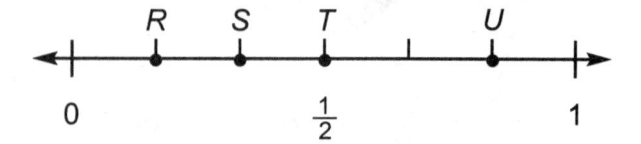

   A Point R C Point T
   B Point S D Point U

(3.1A; 3.1D; 3.1F)

2. Mollie bought a cake and gave half of it to her neighbor.

   Mollie's Cake

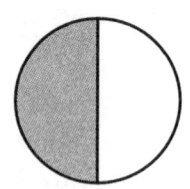

   Jenny bought an identical cake and cut it into 6 equal pieces. Jenny served half of her cake to her family.

   Jenny's Cake

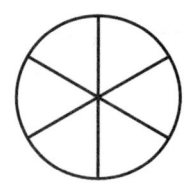

   How many pieces of cake did Jenny serve to her family?

   A 1   C 4
   B 3   D 6

(3.1D; 3.1F)

3. The bar below is divided into 4 equal parts, and $\frac{3}{4}$ of the bar is shaded.

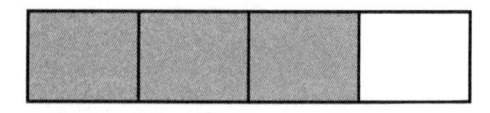

   Which bar shows a fraction equal to $\frac{3}{4}$?

   A 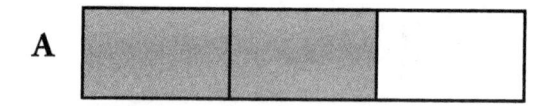
   B 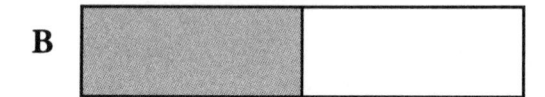
   C 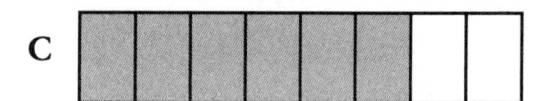
   D

Reporting Category 1
Numerical Representations and Relationships

Exercise 24

3.3F: Represent equivalent fractions with denominators of 2, 3, 4, 6, and 8 using a variety of objects and pictorial models, including number lines (Readiness Standard)

(3.1D; 3.1F)

1. Figures A and B are shaded to show two fractions.

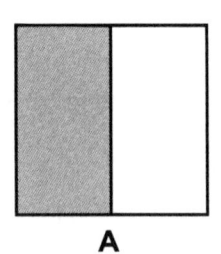

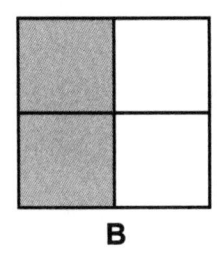

   A   B

   The figures show that—

   A $\frac{1}{4} = \frac{1}{2}$

   B $\frac{1}{2} > \frac{2}{4}$

   C $\frac{2}{4} > \frac{1}{2}$

   D $\frac{1}{2} = \frac{2}{4}$

(3.1D; 3.1F)

2. Which point on the number line below represents $\frac{2}{8}$?

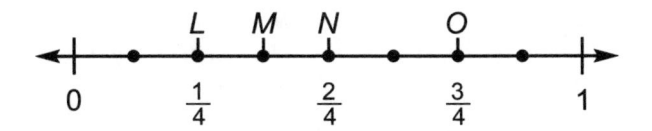

   A Point *L*
   B Point *M*
   C Point *N*
   D Point *O*

(3.1D; 3.1F)

3. The shaded part of figure A represents $\frac{1}{3}$ of the shape.

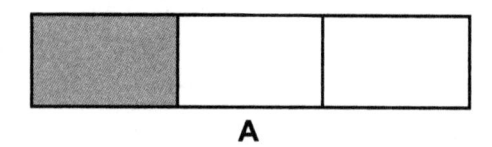

   A

   What fraction of figure B must be shaded to equal $\frac{1}{3}$ of the shape?

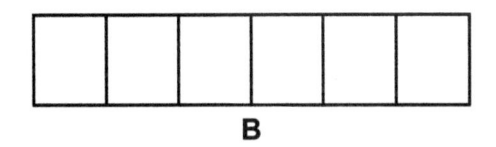

   B

   A $\frac{1}{6}$

   B $\frac{2}{6}$

   C $\frac{3}{6}$

   D $\frac{4}{6}$

Reporting Category 1
Numerical Representations and Relationships

Exercise 25

3.3F: Represent equivalent fractions with denominators of 2, 3, 4, 6, and 8 using a variety of objects and pictorial models, including number lines (Readiness Standard)

(3.1D; 3.1F)

1. Figures A and B are shaded to show two fractions.

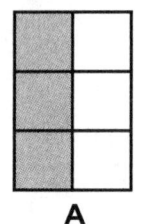

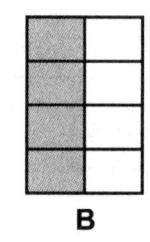

   A   B

   The figures show that—

   A $\frac{1}{6} = \frac{1}{8}$

   B $\frac{3}{6} > \frac{4}{8}$

   C $\frac{3}{6} < \frac{4}{8}$

   D $\frac{3}{6} = \frac{4}{8}$

(3.1D; 3.1F)

2. The number line below is partitioned into fourths and eighths.

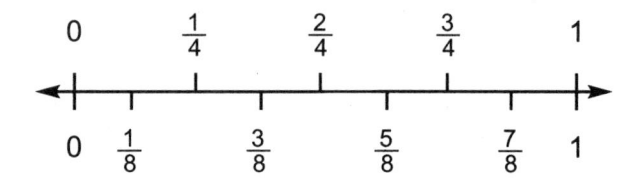

   The number line shows that—

   A $\frac{2}{4} = \frac{3}{8}$

   B $\frac{3}{4} = \frac{6}{8}$

   C $\frac{2}{4} = \frac{5}{8}$

   D $\frac{7}{8} = \frac{3}{4}$

(3.1D; 3.1F)

3. The number line below is partitioned into fourths and sixths.

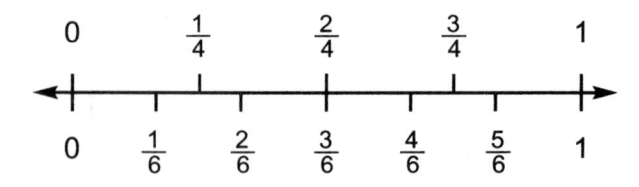

   The number line shows that—

   A $\frac{1}{4} = \frac{1}{6}$

   B $\frac{2}{4} = \frac{4}{6}$

   C $\frac{2}{4} = \frac{3}{6}$

   D $\frac{3}{4} = \frac{5}{6}$

(3.1D; 3.1F)

4. Which point on the number line below represents $\frac{3}{4}$?

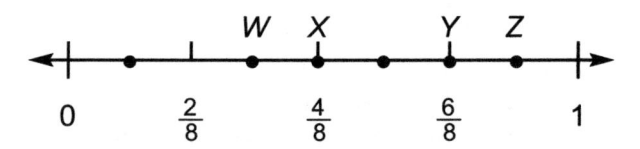

   A Point *W*

   B Point *X*

   C Point *Y*

   D Point *Z*

---

30   STAAR MASTER® Student Practice Book—Math, Grade 3   © ECS Learning Systems, Inc.

Reporting Category 1
Numerical Representations and Relationships

Exercise 26

3.3G: Explain that two fractions are equivalent if and only if they are both represented by the same point on a number line or represent the same portion of a same size whole for an area model (Supporting Standard)

(3.1A; 3.1F; 3.1G)

1. Jenny and Karina each poured one full glass of milk. The shaded portions of the pictures below show the amount of milk each girl drank.

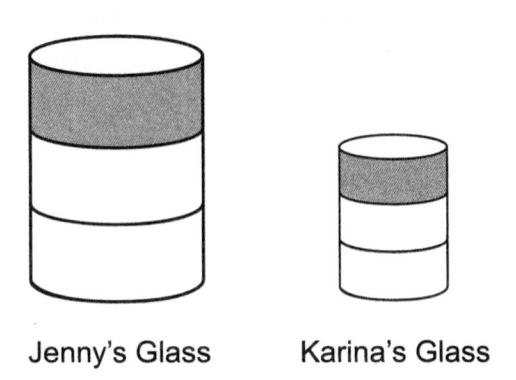

   Jenny's Glass   Karina's Glass

   Which sentence correctly compares the amounts of milk the girls drank?

   A Karina drank more milk than Jenny.
   B Jenny drank more milk than Karina.
   C Each girl drank one full glass of milk.
   D The girls drank the same amount of milk.

(3.1A; 3.1D; 3.1F; 3.1G)

2. David and Jon had money to spend at a school carnival. Each boy spent half of his money on ride tickets. The number lines show how much money the boys spent on ride tickets.

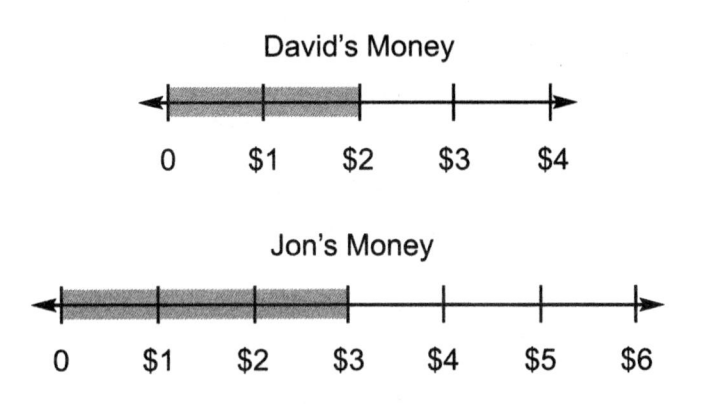

   David's Money
   0   $1 $2 $3 $4

   Jon's Money
   0   $1 $2 $3 $4 $5 $6

   Which sentence correctly compares the amounts of money the boys spent on ride tickets?

   A Each boy spent all of his money.
   B David spent more money than Jon.
   C Jon spent more money than David.
   D The boys spent the same amount of money.

Reporting Category 1
Numerical Representations and Relationships

Exercise 27

3.3G: Explain that two fractions are equivalent if and only if they are both represented by the same point on a number line or represent the same portion of a same size whole for an area model (Supporting Standard)

(3.1A; 3.1F)

1. Grace and Isabel each ate $\frac{1}{4}$ of a pizza. Which set of drawings shows that the girls each ate the same amount of pizza?

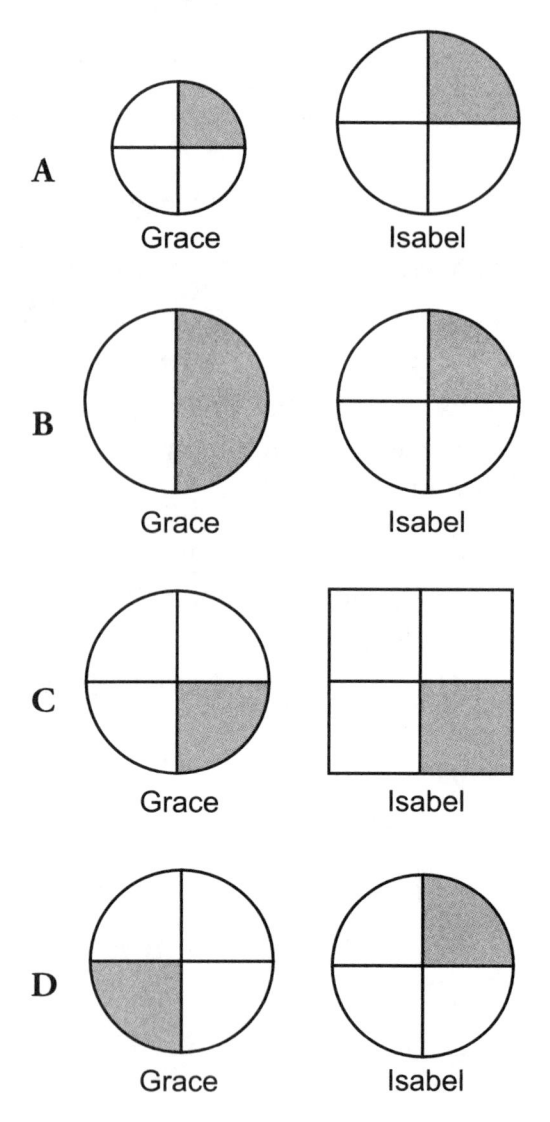

   A   Grace   Isabel

   B   Grace   Isabel

   C   Grace   Isabel

   D   Grace   Isabel

(3.1A; 3.1F; 3.1G)

2. Mrs. Frank and Mrs. Wilson bought the eggs shown below.

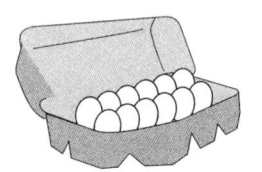

   Mrs. Frank's Eggs   Mrs. Wilson's Eggs

   To bake a cake, Mrs. Frank used $\frac{1}{2}$ of her eggs. To bake brownies, Mrs. Wilson used $\frac{3}{6}$ of her eggs. Which sentence correctly compares the number of eggs the two women used?

   A   Each woman used all the eggs in the carton.

   B   Mrs. Frank used more eggs than Mrs. Wilson.

   C   Mrs. Wilson used more eggs than Mrs. Frank.

   D   The two women each used the same number of eggs.

Reporting Category 1
Numerical Representations and Relationships

Exercise 28

3.3G: Explain that two fractions are equivalent if and only if they are both represented by the same point on a number line or represent the same portion of a same size whole for an area model (Supporting Standard)

(3.1F; 3.1G)

1. The pictures below show two vases. The shaded parts show how much water is in the vases. Vase A is $\frac{3}{4}$ filled. Vase B is $\frac{6}{8}$ filled.

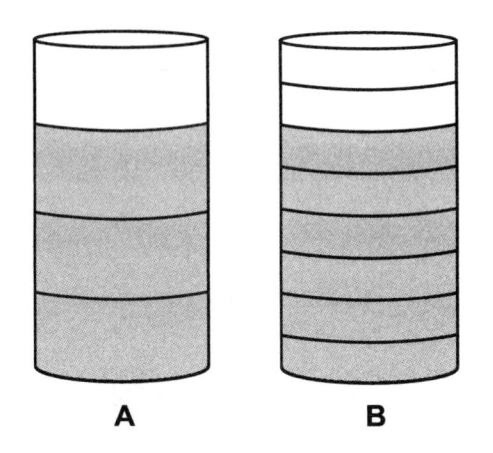

   A   B

   Which sentence correctly compares the amounts of water in the two vases?

   A Both vases are completely full.
   B Vase A has more water than vase B.
   C Vase B has more water than vase A.
   D The vases have the same amount of water.

(3.1A; 3.1D; 3.1F; 3.1G)

2. Reggie and Mike each bike to their friend Todd's house. Each boy stops to rest after biking $\frac{1}{3}$ of the distance to Todd's house. Reggie drew this number line to show how far he biked.

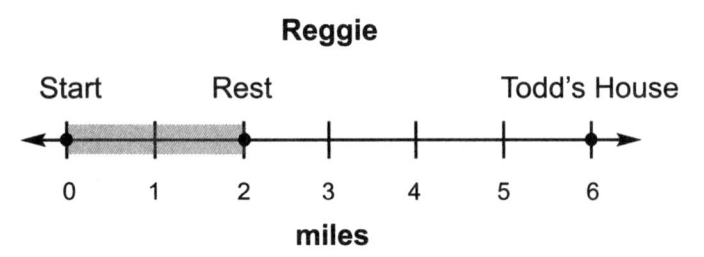

   Reggie
   Start   Rest   Todd's House
   0   1   2   3   4   5   6
   miles

   Mike drew this number line to show how far he biked.

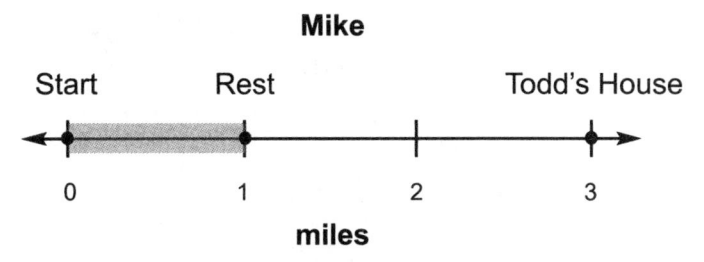

   Mike
   Start   Rest   Todd's House
   0   1   2   3
   miles

   Which sentence correctly compares the distances that the boys bike before stopping to rest?

   A The boys bike the same distance to Todd's house.
   B Reggie bikes farther than Mike before stopping to rest.
   C Mike bikes farther than Reggie before stopping to rest.
   D The boys bike the same distance before stopping to rest.

Reporting Category 1
Numerical Representations and Relationships

Exercise 29

3.3H: Compare two fractions having the same numerator or denominator in problems by reasoning about their sizes and justifying the conclusion using symbols, words, objects, and pictorial models (Readiness Standard)

(3.1D; 3.1F)
1. The models below are shaded to show two fractions.

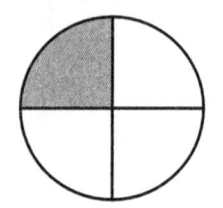

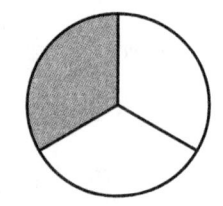

   The models are shaded to show that—

   A $\frac{1}{4} = \frac{1}{3}$

   B $\frac{1}{4} > \frac{1}{3}$

   C $\frac{1}{4} < \frac{1}{3}$

   D $\frac{3}{4} = \frac{2}{3}$

(3.1D; 3.1F)
2. The models below are shaded to show two fractions.

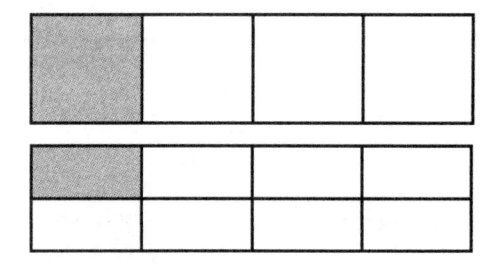

   The models are shaded to show that—

   A $\frac{1}{8} > \frac{1}{4}$

   B $\frac{1}{8} = \frac{1}{4}$

   C $\frac{1}{4} > \frac{1}{8}$

   D $\frac{2}{4} < \frac{2}{8}$

Use the following information to answer questions 3 and 4.

The models below are shaded to show two fractions.

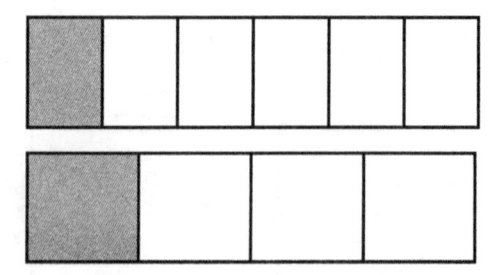

(3.1D; 3.1F)
3. The models are shaded to show that—

   A $\frac{1}{6} > \frac{1}{4}$

   B $\frac{1}{6} < \frac{1}{4}$

   C $\frac{1}{6} = \frac{1}{4}$

   D $\frac{2}{6} = \frac{1}{4}$

(3.1D; 3.1F)
4. Based on the models above, you can also conclude that—

   A $\frac{3}{6} = \frac{2}{4}$

   B $\frac{3}{4} = \frac{3}{6}$

   C $\frac{3}{6} > \frac{3}{4}$

   D $\frac{4}{4} < \frac{4}{6}$

Reporting Category 1
Numerical Representations and Relationships

Exercise 30

3.3H: Compare two fractions having the same numerator or denominator in problems by reasoning about their sizes and justifying the conclusion using symbols, words, objects, and pictorial models (Readiness Standard)

(3.1D; 3.1F)

1. The models below show two circles, each partitioned into equal parts.

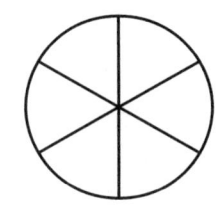

   Based on the models, which expression is true?

   A $\frac{2}{3} = \frac{2}{6}$

   B $\frac{1}{3} < \frac{1}{6}$

   C $\frac{1}{3} = \frac{1}{6}$

   D $\frac{1}{6} < \frac{1}{3}$

(3.1D; 3.1F)

2. Eva and Isa each had 8 new pencils. Eva sharpened $\frac{1}{8}$ of her pencils, and Isa sharpened $\frac{3}{8}$ of her pencils.

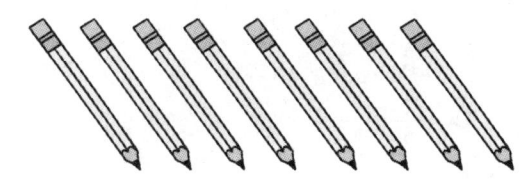

   Which expression correctly compares what fraction of their pencils the girls sharpened?

   A $\frac{3}{8} < \frac{1}{8}$ C $\frac{1}{8} = \frac{3}{8}$

   B $\frac{1}{8} < \frac{3}{8}$ D $\frac{1}{8} > \frac{4}{8}$

(3.1D; 3.1F)

3. The models below are shaded to show two fractions.

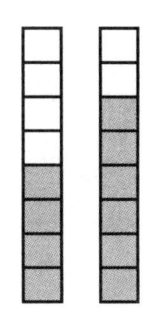

   The shaded portions of the models show that—

   A $\frac{4}{8} > \frac{6}{8}$ C $\frac{4}{8} < \frac{6}{8}$

   B $\frac{4}{4} < \frac{4}{8}$ D $\frac{4}{8} = \frac{6}{8}$

(3.1A; 3.1D; 3.1F)

4. Adam and Keith each cut a strip of paper in math class. Adam cut his paper into 4 equal pieces. Keith cut his paper into 3 equal pieces.

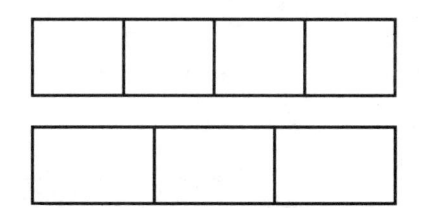

   Based on the models, which expression is true?

   A $\frac{1}{4} > \frac{1}{3}$ C $\frac{2}{3} = \frac{2}{4}$

   B $\frac{1}{4} = \frac{1}{3}$ D $\frac{2}{3} > \frac{2}{4}$

Reporting Category 1
Numerical Representations and Relationships

Exercise 31

3.3H: Compare two fractions having the same numerator or denominator in problems by reasoning about their sizes and justifying the conclusion using symbols, words, objects, and pictorial models (Readiness Standard)

(3.1D; 3.1F)

1. The models below show two squares, each partitioned into equal parts.

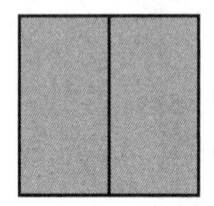

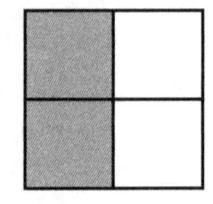

   Based on the models, which expression is true?

   A $\frac{1}{2} > \frac{2}{4}$ C $\frac{2}{2} > \frac{2}{4}$

   B $\frac{1}{2} < \frac{2}{4}$ D $\frac{2}{2} = \frac{2}{4}$

(3.1A; 3.1D; 3.1F)

2. Mina rode her bike $\frac{2}{3}$ of a mile. Olivia rode her bike $\frac{2}{6}$ of a mile.

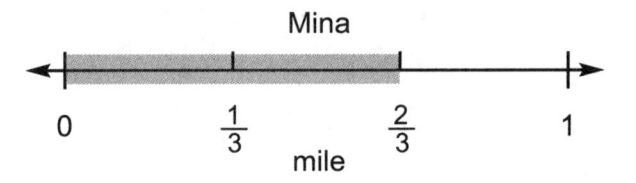

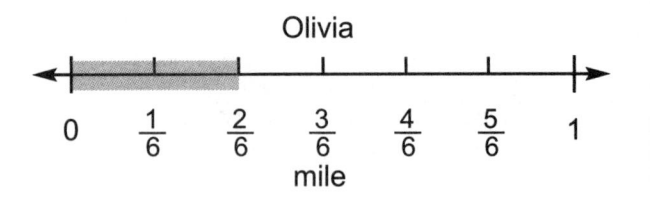

   Mina

   Olivia

   Which expression correctly compares the distances biked by Mina and Olivia?

   A $\frac{2}{3} = \frac{2}{6}$ C $\frac{2}{3} > \frac{2}{6}$

   B $\frac{2}{6} > \frac{2}{3}$ D $\frac{1}{3} < \frac{1}{6}$

(3.1A; 3.1D; 3.1F)

3. Morgan and Tina have the toy cars shown below. Morgan gave $\frac{3}{6}$ of his cars to his little brother. Tina gave $\frac{5}{6}$ of her cars to her little brother.

   Morgan

   Tina

   Which expression correctly compares the fraction of their toy cars that Morgan and Tina gave away?

   A $\frac{3}{6} = \frac{5}{6}$

   B $\frac{5}{6} > \frac{3}{6}$

   C $\frac{5}{6} < \frac{3}{6}$

   D $\frac{1}{5} > \frac{1}{3}$

Reporting Category 1
Numerical Representations and Relationships

Exercise 32

3.3H: Compare two fractions having the same numerator or denominator in problems by reasoning about their sizes and justifying the conclusion using symbols, words, objects, and pictorial models (Readiness Standard)

Use the models below to answer questions 1 and 2.

The models below show three rods, each partitioned into equal parts.

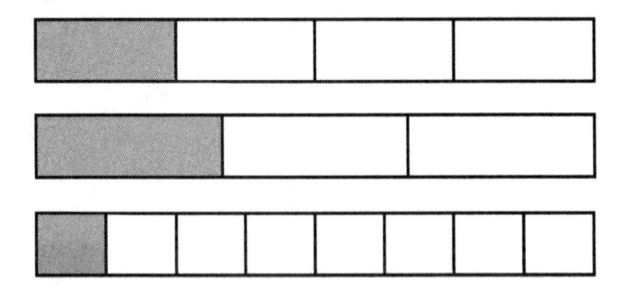

(3.1D; 3.1F)

1. Based on the models, which expression is true?

   A $\frac{1}{4} < \frac{1}{3}$

   B $\frac{1}{3} < \frac{1}{4}$

   C $\frac{1}{4} = \frac{1}{3}$

   D $\frac{2}{4} = \frac{2}{3}$

(3.1D; 3.1F)

2. Based on the models, which expression is true?

   A $\frac{1}{8} > \frac{1}{4}$

   B $\frac{2}{8} > \frac{2}{4}$

   C $\frac{1}{8} = \frac{1}{4}$

   D $\frac{1}{4} > \frac{1}{8}$

(3.1A; 3.1D; 3.1F)

3. Mrs. Jones and Mrs. Guerra each bought cheese to serve at a party. The shaded parts of the models below show how much cheese the party guests ate.

   Mrs. Jones' Cheese

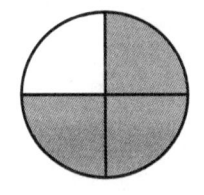

   Mrs. Guerra's Cheese

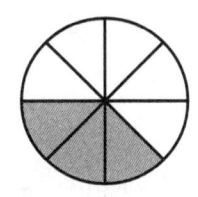

   Based on the models, which expression is true?

   A $\frac{3}{8} < \frac{3}{4}$

   B $\frac{3}{4} < \frac{6}{8}$

   C $\frac{1}{4} = \frac{1}{8}$

   D $\frac{2}{4} = \frac{2}{8}$

Reporting Category 1
Numerical Representations and Relationships

Exercise 33

3.4I: Determine if a number is even or odd using divisibility rules (Supporting Standard)

(3.1D)
1. Which set of figures represents an even number?

   A ☐ ☐ ☐ ☐ ☐

   B ☐ ☐ ☐
      ☐ ☐ ☐

   C ☐ ☐ ☐ ☐
      ☐ ☐ ☐ ☐

   D ☐ ☐ ☐ ☐ ☐
      ☐ ☐ ☐ ☐

2. Which of the following numbers is an odd number?

   A 36
   B 52
   C 78
   D 105

3. Which set of numbers includes only even numbers?

   A 23, 25, 27, 28
   B 32, 34, 36, 38
   C 42, 44, 47, 48
   D 52, 53, 56, 59

(3.1D)
4. Which set of figures represents an odd number?

   A ☐☐ ☐☐

   B ☐☐ ☐☐ ☐☐

   C ☐☐☐ ☐☐☐

   D ☐☐ ☐☐ ☐☐ ☐

(3.1D)
5. Which number cube shows an even number of dots?

   A [cube with 6 dots]

   B [cube with 5 dots]

   C [cube with 3 dots]

   D [cube with 1 dot]

Reporting Category 1
Numerical Representations and Relationships

Exercise 34

3.4I: Determine if a number is even or odd using divisibility rules (Supporting Standard)

(3.1D)

1. Which figure is divided into an even number of sections?

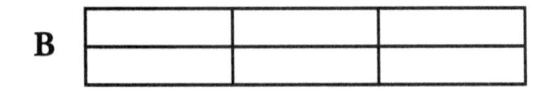

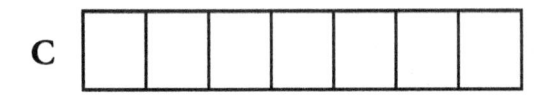

   A
   B
   C
   D

2. Which of the following numbers is an even number?

   A 29
   B 45
   C 63
   D 74

(3.1A; 3.1D)

3. Julia lives on Park Street. Her house's street number is an odd number. Which of the following could be Julia's house?

   2458 4267 5792 6814
   House A House B House C House D

   A House A
   B House B
   C House C
   D House D

4. Which set of numbers includes only odd numbers?

   A 1,025   1,249   1,361   1,683
   B 1,378   1,393   1,595   1,795
   C 1,679   1,712   1,865   1,919
   D 3,333   5,570   6,791   7,960

Reporting Category 1
Numerical Representations and Relationships

Exercise 35

3.7A: Represent fractions of halves, fourths, and eighths as distances from zero on a number line (Supporting Standard)

(3.1D; 3.1F)

1. What fraction is best represented by point A on the number line below?

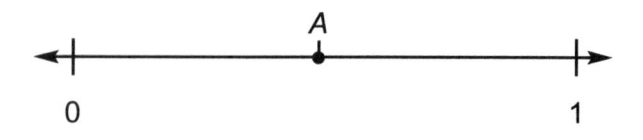

    A $\frac{1}{4}$
    B $\frac{1}{3}$
    C $\frac{1}{2}$
    D $\frac{2}{8}$

(3.1D; 3.1F)

2. What fraction is best represented by point M on the number line below?

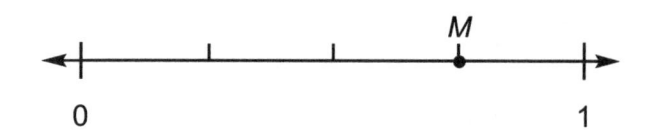

    A $\frac{1}{4}$
    B $\frac{2}{4}$
    C $\frac{3}{4}$
    D $\frac{4}{4}$

(3.1D; 3.1F)

3. On which number line does point R best represent $\frac{5}{8}$?

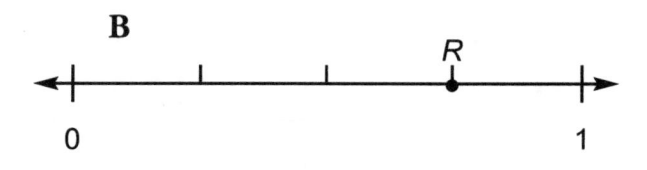

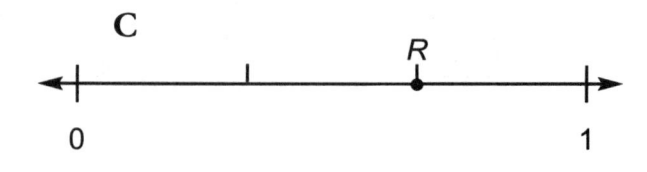

(3.1C; 3.1D; 3.1F)

4. How long is the line drawn above the ruler shown below?

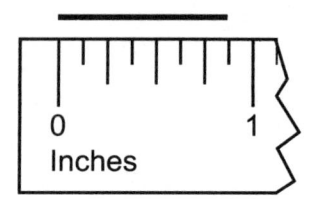

    A $\frac{1}{4}$ inch   C $\frac{3}{4}$ inch
    B $\frac{1}{2}$ inch   D $\frac{7}{8}$ inch

Reporting Category 1
Numerical Representations and Relationships

Exercise 36

3.7A: Represent fractions of halves, fourths, and eighths as distances from zero on a number line (Supporting Standard)

(3.1D; 3.1F)

1. On which number line does point T best represent $\frac{3}{4}$?

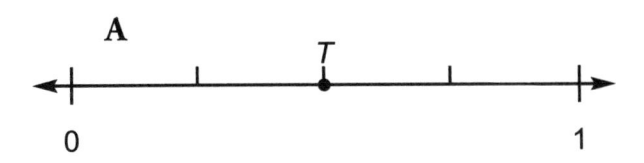

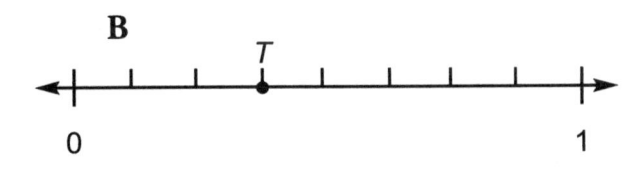

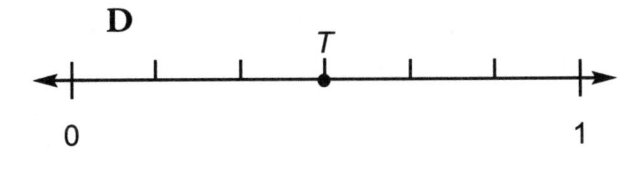

   A

   0 ———T——— 1

   B

   0 —T————— 1

   C

   0 ————T—— 1

   D

   0 ———T——— 1

(3.1C; 3.1D; 3.1F)

2. How long is the line drawn above the ruler shown below?

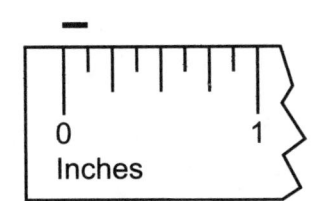

   0 — 1 Inches

   A $\frac{1}{8}$ inch   **C** $\frac{1}{4}$ inch

   B $\frac{2}{8}$ inch   **D** $\frac{1}{2}$ inch

(3.1D; 3.1F)

3. What fraction is best represented by point Q on the number line below?

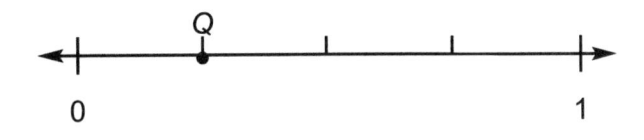

   0 —Q————— 1

   A $\frac{1}{8}$

   B $\frac{1}{4}$

   C $\frac{1}{3}$

   D $\frac{2}{4}$

(3.1C; 3.1D; 3.1F)

4. How long is the line drawn above the ruler shown below?

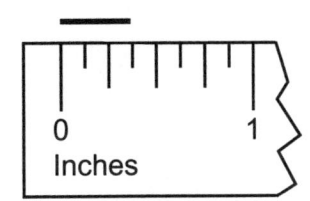

   0 — 1 Inches

   A $\frac{1}{4}$ inch

   B $\frac{1}{3}$ inch

   C $\frac{3}{8}$ inch

   D $\frac{1}{2}$ inch

Reporting Category 2
Computations and Algebraic Relationships

3.4   A. Solve with fluency one-step and two-step problems involving addition and subtraction within 1,000 using strategies based on place value, properties of operations, and the relationship between addition and subtraction (Readiness Standard)

B. Round to the nearest 10 or 100 or use compatible numbers to estimate solutions to addition and subtraction problems (Supporting Standard)

D. Determine the total number of objects when equally sized groups of objects are combined or arranged in arrays up to 10 by 10 (Supporting Standard)

E. Represent multiplication facts by using a variety of approaches such as repeated addition, equal-sized groups, arrays, area models, equal jumps on a number line, and skip counting (Supporting Standard)

F. Recall facts to multiply up to 10 by 10 with automaticity, and recall the corresponding division facts (Supporting Standard)

G. Use strategies and algorithms, including the standard algorithm, to multiply a two-digit number by a one-digit number. Strategies may include mental math, partial products, and the commutative, associative, and distributive properties (Supporting Standard)

H. Determine the number of objects in each group when a set of objects is partitioned into equal shares or a set of objects is shared equally (Supporting Standard)

J. Determine a quotient using the relationship between multiplication and division (Supporting Standard)

K. Solve one-step and two-step problems involving multiplication and division within 100 using strategies based on objects; pictorial models, including arrays, area models, and equal groups; properties of operations; or recall of facts (Readiness Standard)

3.5   A. Represent one- and two-step problems involving addition and subtraction of whole numbers to 1,000 using pictorial models, number lines, and equations (Readiness Standard)

B. Represent and solve one- and two-step multiplication and division problems within 100 using arrays, strip diagrams, and equations (Readiness Standard)

C. Describe a multiplication expression as a comparison such as 3 × 24 represents 3 times as much as 24 (Supporting Standard)

D. Determine the unknown whole number in a multiplication or division equation relating three whole numbers when the unknown is either a missing factor or product (Supporting Standard)

E. Represent real-world relationships using number pairs in a table and verbal descriptions (Readiness Standard)

Reporting Category 2
Computations and Algebraic Relationships

Exercise 1

3.4A: Solve with fluency one-step and two-step problems involving addition and subtraction within 1,000 using strategies based on place value, properties of operations, and the relationship between addition and subtraction (Readiness Standard)

(3.1A; 3.1B; 3.1D; 3.1E)

1. There are 5 malls near Mr. Wolford's home. The table below shows how many stores are in each mall.

Mall Stores

Mall	Number of Stores
Bellview	27
City Center	104
Davidson	32
Edmunds	58
Franktown	109

How many more stores are in City Center Mall than in Edmunds Mall?

A 162
B 56
C 54
D 46

(3.1A; 3.1B)

2. The Morris family went to the beach. They collected 425 shells in all. Zach collected 160 shells, and Emily collected 128 shells. How many shells did the rest of the family collect?

A 137
B 265
C 297
D 713

(3.1A; 3.1B)

3. Annie collected 87 leaves, Sara collected 43 leaves, and Libby collected 196 leaves. How many more leaves did Libby collect than Annie and Sara combined?

A 66
B 109
C 153
D 326

(3.1A; 3.1B)

4. Mrs. Miller's class sold 125 boxes of cookies. Mr. Toler's class sold 128 boxes. Mrs. Burns' class sold 5 more boxes than Mrs. Miller's class. How many boxes did the three classes sell in all?

Record your answer in the boxes. Then fill in the bubbles. Be sure to use the correct place value.

Reporting Category 2
Computations and Algebraic Relationships

Exercise 2

3.4A: Solve with fluency one-step and two-step problems involving addition and subtraction within 1,000 using strategies based on place value, properties of operations, and the relationship between addition and subtraction (Readiness Standard)

(3.1A; 3.1B)

1. A third-grade class has a goal of reading 100 pages during Silent Reading this week. Nicole read 15 pages. Molly read 12 pages. How many more pages does the class need to read to reach its goal?

   A 3
   B 27
   C 73
   D 127

(3.1A; 3.1B)

2. Class A saved 110 bottles to recycle. Class B saved 320 bottles. Class C saved 215 bottles. The school wants to save 950 bottles in all. How many more bottles does the school need to save?

   A 305
   B 415
   C 520
   D 645

(3.1A; 3.1B)

3. Sean won 137 tickets at the county fair. His friend won 129 tickets. Sean's dad won 45 tickets. How many more tickets did Sean and his friend win together than Sean's dad?

   Record your answer in the boxes. Then fill in the bubbles. Be sure to use the correct place value.

(3.1A; 3.1B; 3.1D; 3.1E)

4. The town of Belleville has 3 schools with 500 students altogether.

   Belleville Schools

School	Number of Students
Elm Grove	134
Maple Knoll	199
Oak Meadow	

   How many students does Oak Meadow School have?

   A 167
   B 177
   C 267
   D 333

(3.1A; 3.1B)

5. Amy and her sisters counted the number of red cars they saw on a trip. Amy counted 62 red cars, Liz counted 81 red cars, and Beth counted 73 red cars. How many total red cars did Amy and Beth count?

   A 216
   B 154
   C 143
   D 135

Reporting Category 2
Computations and Algebraic Relationships

Exercise 3

3.4A: Solve with fluency one-step and two-step problems involving addition and subtraction within 1,000 using strategies based on place value, properties of operations, and the relationship between addition and subtraction (Readiness Standard)

(3.1A; 3.1B)

1. A group of students made a list of where they went most often during summer vacation. Fourteen students went to the museum most often, 10 students went to the swimming pool most often, and 12 students went to the park most often. How many more students went to the museum and the park most often than to the swimming pool?

   A 12
   B 16
   C 26
   D 36

(3.1A; 3.1B; 3.1D; 3.1E)

2. A class made a chart of the rainfall in the students' town for three years.

   Rainfall

Month	Rain (in inches)
2001	15
2002	28
2003	14

   What is the difference in rainfall between the month with the greatest amount and the month with the least amount of rain?

   A 1 in.
   B 13 in.
   C 14 in.
   D 15 in.

(3.1A; 3.1B; 3.1D; 3.1E)

3. Ski Valley is a popular place for vacations. The chart below shows the snowfall in Ski Valley last winter.

   Snowfall

Month	Snow (in inches)
November	35
December	40
January	55
February	55

   What is the total amount of snow for the two months with the greatest snowfall?

   A 75 in.   C 110 in.
   B 90 in.   D 185 in.

(3.1A; 3.1B)

4. The Yum-Yum Snack Shop sells cookies, ice cream cones, fruit cups, and bags of nuts. Last week, the following items were sold: 132 cookies, 147 ice cream cones, 121 fruit cups, and 155 bags of nuts. How many total cookies and fruit cups were sold?

   Record your answer in the boxes. Then fill in the bubbles. Be sure to use the correct place value.

Reporting Category 2
Computations and Algebraic Relationships

Exercise 4

3.4A: Solve with fluency one-step and two-step problems involving addition and subtraction within 1,000 using strategies based on place value, properties of operations, and the relationship between addition and subtraction (Readiness Standard)

(3.1A; 3.1B)

1. Wyatt and his friends counted the number of hermit crabs they saw at the beach. Wyatt saw 134 hermit crabs, Seth saw 201 hermit crabs, and Jon saw 98 hermit crabs. How many more hermit crabs did Wyatt and Jon see together than Seth?

   A 31
   B 98
   C 165
   D 237

(3.1A; 3.1B)

2. Thomas wants to save $195 to buy a new bike. If he saves $15 one week and $12 the next week, how many more dollars will he need to save?

   Record your answer in the boxes. Then fill in the bubbles. Be sure to use the correct place value.

(3.1A; 3.1B)

3. Rick bought 95 baseball cards and 75 basketball cards. Then, he bought 40 more baseball cards. How many total baseball cards did Rick buy?

   A 55
   B 135
   C 170
   D 210

(3.1A; 3.1B)

4. Kelly earned 215 points in a game. Mike earned 10 points less than Kelly. Jim earned 20 points more than Kelly. Molly earned 100 points more than Mike. Which list shows the children's names in order from least to greatest points earned in the game?

   A Kelly, Mike, Jim, Molly
   B Mike, Kelly, Jim, Molly
   C Molly, Mike, Jim, Kelly
   D Jim, Kelly, Mike, Molly

(3.1A; 3.1B)

5. Mr. Trevino drove 760 miles during May and 810 miles during June. He normally drives 900 miles each month. How many more miles did Mr. Trevino drive in June than in May?

   A 50
   B 90
   C 140
   D 150

Reporting Category 2
Computations and Algebraic Relationships

Exercise 5

3.4A: Solve with fluency one-step and two-step problems involving addition and subtraction within 1,000 using strategies based on place value, properties of operations, and the relationship between addition and subtraction (Readiness Standard)

(3.1A; 3.1B)

1. Joel ran 3 miles, and his dad ran 5 miles. Joel's uncle ran 4 miles farther than Joel and his father ran together. How many miles did the three run in all?

   A 12
   B 15
   C 20
   D 22

(3.1A; 3.1B)

2. Ethan has 65 baseball cards. Jim has 94 baseball cards. Jim's brother has the same number of cards as Jim. How many more baseball cards do Jim and his brother have than Ethan?

   A 29
   B 94
   C 123
   D 159

(3.1A; 3.1B)

3. Dallas is 327 miles away from Halia's house, and Houston is 219 miles away. How much farther away from Halia's house is Dallas than Houston?

   A 18 mi
   B 22 mi
   C 108 mi
   D 112 mi

(3.1A; 3.1B; 3.1D; 3.1E)

4. Students voted on their favorite reward, as shown below.

   Rewards

Reward	Votes
Food	325
Movie	562
Games	428

   How many more votes were for a movie than for games?

   A 103
   B 134
   C 237
   D 990

(3.1A; 3.1B)

5. A bookstore received 505 orders for a new children's book. The store filled 130 orders on Monday and 145 orders on Tuesday. How many more orders did the store need to fill after Tuesday?

   Record your answer in the boxes. Then fill in the bubbles. Be sure to use the correct place value.

48 STAAR MASTER® Student Practice Book—Math, Grade 3

Reporting Category 2
Computations and Algebraic Relationships

Exercise 6

3.4B: Round to the nearest 10 or 100 or use compatible numbers to estimate solutions to addition and subtraction problems (Supporting Standard)

(3.1A; 3.1B; 3.1D)

1. Juan kept a log of the time he spent reading during June and July. In June, he spent 337 minutes reading. He recorded 482 minutes in his log for July. Which number sentence best shows about how many more minutes he spent reading in July than in June?

   A 340 + 480 = 820
   B 330 + 480 = 810
   C 480 − 340 = 140
   D 500 − 400 = 100

(3.1A; 3.1B; 3.1D; 3.1E)

2. Jeff kept track of the number of people who saw the school play one weekend. The numbers are shown in the table below.

   School Play Attendance

Day	Number of People
Friday	312
Saturday	362
Sunday	291

   Rounded to the nearest hundred, about how many people saw the school play?

   A 800
   B 900
   C 1,000
   D 1,100

(3.1A; 3.1B; 3.1D; 3.1E)

3. John Thomas Elementary School collected pennies for soldiers. The table below shows the number of pennies collected in three grades.

   Pennies Collected for Soldiers

Grade	Number of Pennies
Third	3,498
Fourth	2,003
Fifth	4,826

   Which of the following shows the best estimate for the total number of pennies collected by these three grades?

   A 3,000 + 2,000 + 4,000
   B 3,500 + 2,500 + 5,000
   C 3,500 + 2,000 + 4,800
   D 4,000 + 2,000 + 5,000

(3.1A; 3.1B)

4. At the school science fair Egg Drop, Harold's egg dropped 133 inches without breaking. Julie's egg dropped 209 inches without breaking. What is the best estimate of how many more inches Julie's egg dropped?

   A 30
   B 70
   C 90
   D 100

Reporting Category 2
Computations and Algebraic Relationships

Exercise 7

3.4B: Round to the nearest 10 or 100 or use compatible numbers to estimate solutions to addition and subtraction problems (Supporting Standard)

(3.1A; 3.1B; 3.1D; 3.1E)

1. Coach Alexander gives yearly fitness tests to the students at Montgomery Intermediate School. The table below shows the number of tests he gave last year.

Fitness Tests Given

Grade	Number of Students
4	466
5	443
6	496

Which number sentence shows the best estimate of how many fitness tests Coach Alexander gave last year?

A 400 + 400 + 500 = 1,300
B 450 + 450 + 400 = 1,300
C 470 + 440 + 500 = 1,410
D 500 + 500 + 500 = 1,500

(3.1A; 3.1B; 3.1D; 3.1E)

2. Matt bought 2 packages of gum for 64 cents each. He also bought a candy bar for 75 cents. Which expression shows the best estimate for how much money Matt spent?

A 60 + 80
B 60 + 70 + 70
C 60 + 60 + 80
D 70 + 70 + 80

(3.1A; 3.1B; 3.1D)

3. Sawyer Elementary School has 193 boys and 231 girls. Which expression shows the best estimate for the total number of students that attend Sawyer Elementary School?

A 200 + 300
B 200 + 200
C 100 + 200
D 100 + 100

(3.1A; 3.1B)

4. The Tyler Rose Garden has 421 pink rose bushes, 385 red rose bushes, and 179 yellow rose bushes. Which is the best estimate of how many more pink rose bushes than yellow rose bushes the garden has?

A 150
B 240
C 260
D 300

(3.1A; 3.1B)

5. Davis Plant Farm has 287 red and pink tulip plants to sell in the spring. There are 195 pink tulip plants. Which is the best estimate of the number of red tulip plants?

A 75
B 100
C 150
D 200

Reporting Category 2
Computations and Algebraic Relationships

Exercise 8

3.4B: Round to the nearest 10 or 100 or use compatible numbers to estimate solutions to addition and subtraction problems (Supporting Standard)

(3.1A; 3.1B)

1. Mr. Ross has 986 pounds of dirt. He sells 319 pounds to Store A and 267 pounds to Store B. Which is the best estimate of how much dirt Mr. Ross has left?

   A 400 pounds
   B 420 pounds
   C 500 pounds
   D 590 pounds

(3.1A; 3.1B; 3.1D; 3.1E)

2. A stand at the fall carnival sold lemonade. The table below shows how many cups of lemonade were sold during the three-day event.

   Lemonade Sales

Day	Cups Sold
Friday	148
Saturday	195
Sunday	102

   Which number sentence shows the best estimate of how many cups of lemonade were sold during the fall carnival?

   A 140 + 200 + 100 = 440
   B 150 + 200 + 100 = 450
   C 200 + 200 + 100 = 500
   D 200 + 200 + 200 = 600

(3.1A; 3.1B)

3. Elm Elementary School collected newspaper for recycling. Mr. Smith's class collected 124 pounds, Mr. Johnson's class collected 257 pounds, and Mrs. Jones' class collected 312 pounds. About how many pounds of newspaper did all three classes collect?

   A 600
   B 700
   C 800
   D 900

(3.1A; 3.1B)

4. Brock has $10 to spend on toys. He buys each toy shown below.

   79¢ $1.19 $4.69

   Which is the best estimate for the amount of money Brock has left after buying the toys?

   A $2.00
   B $2.50
   C $3.00
   D $4.00

Reporting Category 2
Computations and Algebraic Relationships

Exercise 9

3.4B: Round to the nearest 10 or 100 or use compatible numbers to estimate solutions to addition and subtraction problems (Supporting Standard)

(3.1A; 3.1B)

1. Mr. George weighs 212 pounds. If he loses 33 pounds, about how much would he weigh after losing the weight?

   A 160 pounds
   B 180 pounds
   C 200 pounds
   D 240 pounds

(3.1A; 3.1B; 3.1D)

2. Jacob counted how many cars he saw while riding the bus to school. The table below shows how many of each color he saw.

   Cars Jacob Saw

Color	Number
Red	18
Black	23
Blue	14
Silver	27

   Which is the best estimate of how many cars Jacob saw on his way to school?

   A 60
   B 80
   C 90
   D 100

(3.1A; 3.1B; 3.1D)

3. Bobby earned $27 for mowing the lawn. He earned $12 for taking out the trash for a week. Which expression shows the best way to find about how much money Bobby earned altogether?

   A 10 + 10
   B 20 + 10
   C 30 + 10
   D 30 + 20

(3.1A; 3.1B; 3.1D)

4. Charles delivers 164 newspapers on Saturday and 272 newspapers on Sunday. Which expressions shows the best way to find about how many newspapers he delivers on both days?

   A 100 + 200
   B 100 + 160
   C 200 + 160
   D 200 + 300

(3.1A; 3.1B)

5. Mrs. Austin drove 76 miles from her home to a hotel. Then, she drove 18 miles from the hotel to her sister's house. Which is the best estimate for the total distance she drove?

   A 60 miles
   B 70 miles
   C 80 miles
   D 100 miles

Reporting Category 2
Computations and Algebraic Relationships

Exercise 10

3.4D: Determine the total number of objects when equally sized groups of objects are combined or arranged in arrays up to 10 by 10 (Supporting Standard)

(3.1A; 3.1D; 3.1E)

1. Tony bought 3 strips of his school picture. Each strip had 4 individual pictures.

   How many individual pictures did Tony buy?

   A 3
   B 4
   C 9
   D 12

(3.1A; 3.1D; 3.1E)

2. When Sophie makes a batch of cookies, she uses 3 cups of flour. If she decides to make 6 batches of cookies for a bake sale, which of the following can be used to find how many cups of flour Sophie needs?

   A, B,  C, 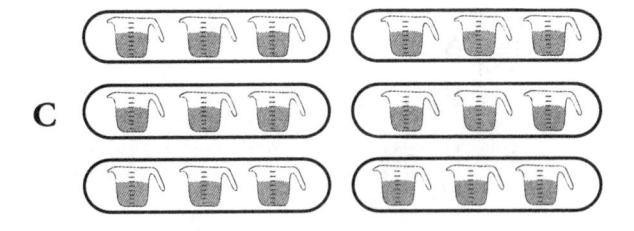 D

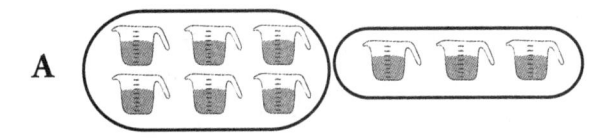

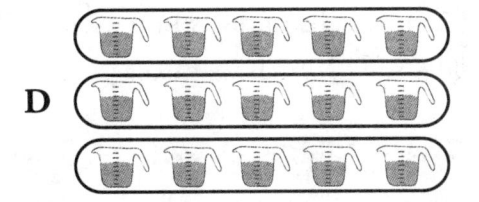

Reporting Category 2
Computations and Algebraic Relationships

Exercise 11

3.4D: Determine the total number of objects when equally sized groups of objects are combined or arranged in arrays up to 10 by 10 (Supporting Standard)

(3.1A; 3.1E)

1. Mrs. Jones bought paper plates in packages like the one shown below.

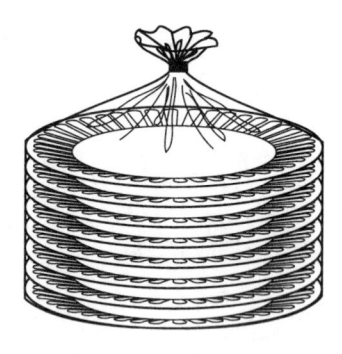

   If she bought 7 packages of the plates, how many paper plates did Mrs. Jones buy?

   A 8
   B 15
   C 56
   D 63

(3.1A; 3.1D)

2. A store sells oranges in packages like the ones shown below.

   Eddie bought 4 packages of oranges. How many oranges did Eddie buy?

   A 4
   B 8
   C 12
   D 16

(3.1A; 3.1E)

3. A worker must replace the legs on 5 tables like the one shown below.

   How many table legs must the worker replace in all?

   A 25
   B 20
   C 9
   D 5

(3.1A; 3.1D)

4. Morgan has 6 stacks of nickels, with 6 nickels in each stack.

   What is the total number of nickels in the 6 stacks?

   A 6
   B 12
   C 30
   D 36

Reporting Category 2
Computations and Algebraic Relationships

Exercise 12

3.4D: Determine the total number of objects when equally sized groups of objects are combined or arranged in arrays up to 10 by 10 (Supporting Standard)

(3.1A; 3.1E)

1. Mrs. Rosewood bought 3 notebooks for each of her 9 grandchildren.

   How many notebooks did Mrs. Rosewood buy in all?

   A 12
   B 24
   C 27
   D 30

(3.1A; 3.1D)

2. For P.E. class, Sally set out kickballs as shown in the picture below.

   How many kickballs did Sally set out for P.E. class?

   A 3
   B 6
   C 15
   D 18

(3.1A; 3.1D)

3. A chef used the eggs shown below to make pound cakes.

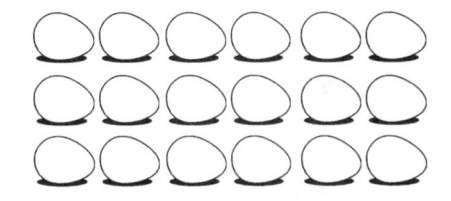

   How many eggs did the chef use to make the pound cakes?

   A 6
   B 18
   C 24
   D 30

(3.1A; 3.1D)

4. A principal gave a bunch of balloons to the spelling bee champion at each grade level.

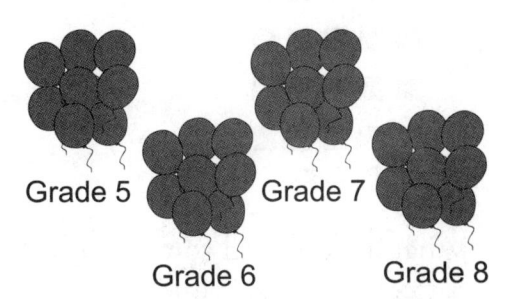

   Grade 5   Grade 7
   Grade 6   Grade 8

   What was the total number of balloons given by the principal?

   A 4
   B 8
   C 24
   D 32

Reporting Category 2
Computations and Algebraic Relationships

Exercise 13

3.4E: Represent multiplication facts by using a variety of approaches such as repeated addition, equal-sized groups, arrays, area models, equal jumps on a number line, and skip counting (Supporting Standard)

(3.1D)

1. Which of the following best represents 4 × 5?

   A ▪▪▪▪
      ▪▪▪▪▪

   B ▪▪▪▪▪
      ▪▪▪▪▪
      ▪▪▪▪▪
      ▪▪▪▪▪

   C ▪▪▪▪
      ▪▪▪▪
      ▪▪▪▪
      ▪▪▪▪

   D ▪▪▪▪▪
      ▪▪▪▪▪
      ▪▪▪▪▪
      ▪▪▪▪▪
      ▪▪▪▪▪

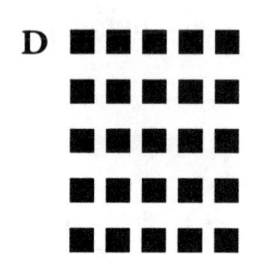

2. What number will come next if the pattern below continues?

   3, 6, 9, 12, _____

   A 10
   B 13
   C 14
   D 15

(3.1D)

3. Which multiplication fact do the arrows on the number line below best represent?

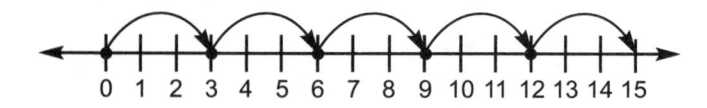

   A 3 × 3 = 9
   B 4 × 3 = 12
   C 5 × 3 = 15
   D 6 × 3 = 18

(3.1D)

4. Which multiplication fact does the area model below best represent?

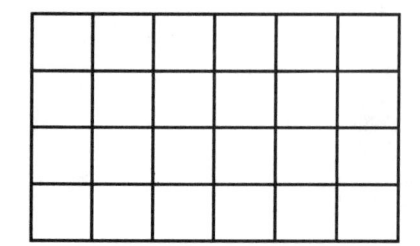

   A 4 × 4 = 16
   B 4 × 5 = 20
   C 4 × 6 = 24
   D 6 × 6 = 36

Reporting Category 2
Computations and Algebraic Relationships

Exercise 14

3.4E: Represent multiplication facts by using a variety of approaches such as repeated addition, equal-sized groups, arrays, area models, equal jumps on a number line, and skip counting (Supporting Standard)

(3.1A)
1. A clerk sells crayons in boxes like the one shown below.

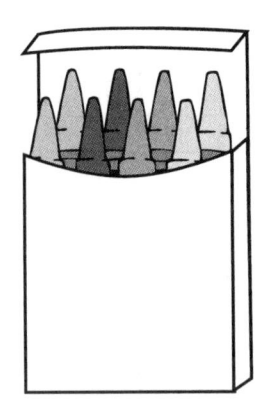

 The clerk wants to know the total number of crayons he sells. Which list shows numbers that he might count to find the answer?

 A 0, 12, 20, 24, 32
 B 8, 14, 20, 26, 32
 C 8, 16, 24, 32, 40
 D 8, 16, 36, 62, 128

(3.1A; 3.1D)
2. The array below shows several fish.

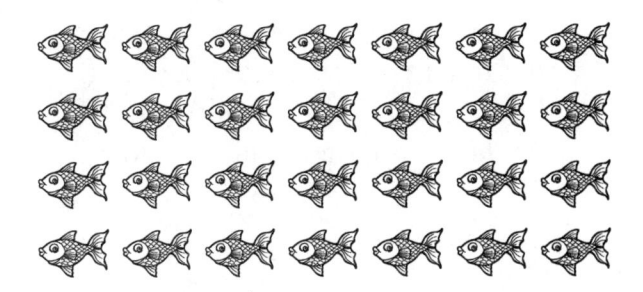

 Which multiplication fact does the array best represent?

 A 6 × 4 = 24   C 2 × 14 = 28
 B 7 × 4 = 28   D 1 × 28 = 28

(3.1D)
3. Which multiplication fact does the area model below best represent?

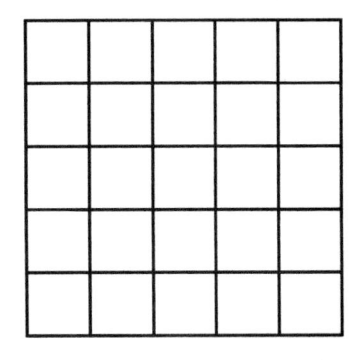

 A 4 × 4 = 16
 B 4 × 5 = 20
 C 5 × 5 = 25
 D 5 × 6 = 30

(3.1A; 3.1D)
4. Miss Clark bought a container of 18 eggs. How were the eggs most likely arranged in the container?

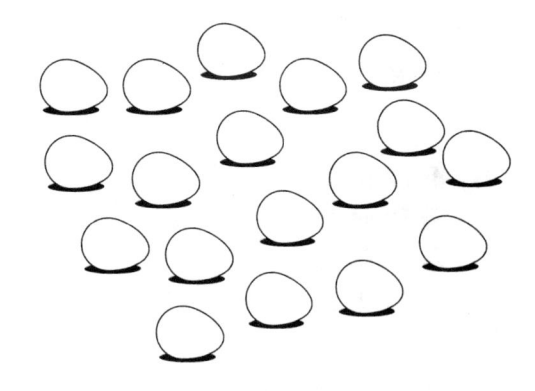

 A 1 row of 18 eggs
 B 3 rows with 6 eggs in each row
 C 4 rows with 4 eggs in each row
 D 2 rows with 6 eggs in each row

© ECS Learning Systems, Inc.

STAAR MASTER® Student Practice Book—Math, Grade 3

Reporting Category 2
Computations and Algebraic Relationships

Exercise 15

3.4E: Represent multiplication facts by using a variety of approaches such as repeated addition, equal-sized groups, arrays, area models, equal jumps on a number line, and skip counting (Supporting Standard)

(3.1A; 3.1F)

1. Erin arranged her shells in 2 rows with 10 shells in each row. Then she arranged them in other even rows. Which way is **NOT** an arrangement she could have made?

   A 5 rows with 4 shells in each row
   B 6 rows with 2 shells in each row
   C 4 rows with 5 shells in each row
   D 10 rows with 2 shells in each row

(3.1D)

2. Which arrangement below could be used to show 4 × 4 = 16?

   A ▪▪▪▪ ▪▪▪▪
   B (4×4 square array)
   C (6 squares over 4 squares)
   D (two rows of 7 squares)

(3.1D)

3. Which area model best represents the multiplication fact 4 × 7 = 28?

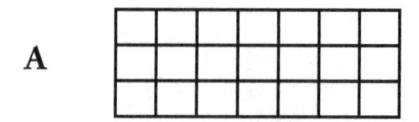

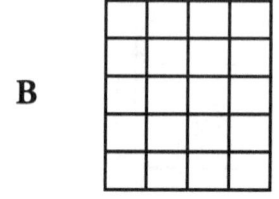

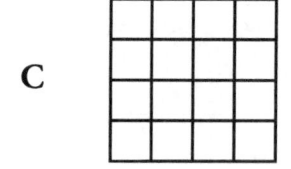

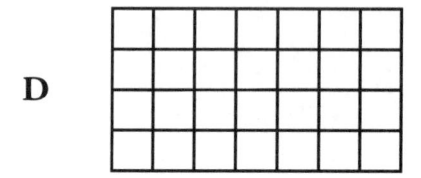

   A (grid)
   B (grid)
   C (grid)
   D (grid)

(3.1A; 3.1F)

4. At a fun park, a worker collects 5 tokens from each person who rides the roller coaster. To keep track of how many tokens he collected, the worker wrote the numbers below.

   $$5 + 5 + 5 + 5 + 5 + 5 + 5$$

   Which is another way the worker could have written the same amount?

   A 57   C 7 × 5
   B 5 + 7   D 7 × 7

Reporting Category 2
Computations and Algebraic Relationships

Exercise 16

3.4F: Recall facts to multiply up to 10 by 10 with automaticity, and recall the corresponding division facts (Supporting Standard)

(3.1F)

1. Which of the following numbers would make both number sentences below correct?

    5 × ☐ = 35   ☐ × 8 = 56

    A 6
    B 7
    C 8
    D 9

2. Which expression below has a product of 36?

    A 4 × 8
    B 6 × 5
    C 6 × 7
    D 4 × 9

3. Which two expressions have a product of 18?

    A 2 × 9 and 3 × 6
    B 2 × 9 and 4 × 6
    C 3 × 8 and 2 × 7
    D 3 × 8 and 4 × 6

(3.1F)

4. Which of the following will make the number sentences below correct?

    40 ÷ △ = 8   40 ÷ ☐ = 4

    A △ = 6, ☐ = 10
    B △ = 5, ☐ = 11
    C △ = 10, ☐ = 5
    D △ = 5, ☐ = 10

(3.1A; 3.1B)

5. Jonathan's mom baked 9 pans of cupcakes for his birthday party. Each pan makes 9 cupcakes. How many cupcakes did Jonathan's mom bake?

    Record your answer in the boxes. Then fill in the bubbles. Be sure to use the correct place value.

Reporting Category 2
Computations and Algebraic Relationships

Exercise 17

3.4F: Recall facts to multiply up to 10 by 10 with automaticity, and recall the corresponding division facts (Supporting Standard)

(3.1A; 3.1B)

1. Tricia is sewing outfits for her dolls. Each outfit requires 3 yards of fabric. How many yards of fabric does Tricia need if she is going to make 7 outfits?

   A 18
   B 21
   C 24
   D 27

(3.1A; 3.1B)

2. The 54 members of an orchestra sit in rows. An equal number of members sit in each row. How many rows of orchestra members could there be?

   A 5
   B 6
   C 7
   D 8

(3.1A; 3.1B)

3. Mrs. Ali baked 64 cookies for a party. She served an equal number of cookies on each of several plates. If she served all the cookies, how many plates could she have used?

   A 5
   B 7
   C 8
   D 9

(3.1A; 3.1B)

4. A teacher has 36 students in her class. She must send the students to the library in 6 small groups. If the teacher sends the students in groups of equal size, how many students will be in each group?

   Record your answer in the boxes. Then fill in the bubbles. Be sure to use the correct place value.

(3.1A; 3.1B)

5. A park has 63 lampposts along several sidewalks. If there are an equal number of lights along each sidewalk, how many lampposts could be along each sidewalk?

   A 5
   B 6
   C 7
   D 8

Reporting Category 2
Computations and Algebraic Relationships

Exercise 18

3.4F: Recall facts to multiply up to 10 by 10 with automaticity, and recall the corresponding division facts (Supporting Standard)

1. Which expression has a product of 42?

   A 7 × 8
   B 7 × 6
   C 6 × 6
   D 6 × 8

(3.1F)

2. Which of the following will make the number sentences below correct?

   $36 \div \square = 4 \quad 48 \div \triangle = 6$

   A $\square = 8; \triangle = 8$
   B $\square = 9; \triangle = 9$
   C $\square = 9; \triangle = 8$
   D $\square = 9; \triangle = 7$

(3.1F)

3. Which digit will make both number sentences correct?

   $4 \times \square = 32 \quad 72 \div \square = 9$

   A 6
   B 7
   C 8
   D 9

4. Which two expressions have a product of 24?

   A 3 × 8 and 2 × 9
   B 4 × 4 and 5 × 6
   C 4 × 6 and 8 × 3
   D 6 × 3 and 4 × 8

(3.1A; 3.1B)

5. Tina bought 49 tulip bulbs to plant in her garden. She planted an equal number of tulips in each of 7 rows. How many tulips did Tina plant in each row?

   A 5
   B 6
   C 7
   D 8

Reporting Category 2
Computations and Algebraic Relationships

Exercise 19

3.4G: Use strategies and algorithms, including the standard algorithm, to multiply a two-digit number by a one-digit number. Strategies may include mental math, partial products, and the commutative, associative, and distributive properties (Supporting Standard)

(3.1A; 3.1B)

1. Sheila's mother buys paper cups that come in a package of 18 cups. If Sheila's mother buys 7 packages for a party, how many cups will she buy?

   A 25
   B 76
   C 126
   D 134

(3.1A; 3.1B)

2. Oranges are sold in boxes of 24 oranges. How many oranges will be in 7 boxes?

   A 148
   B 158
   C 168
   D 172

(3.1A; 3.1B)

3. The PTA president bought 9 boxes of cookies for a meeting. Each box had 42 cookies. How many cookies did the PTA president buy?

   A 368
   B 378
   C 388
   D 398

(3.1A; 3.1B)

4. A factory packs 24 pencils in each box.

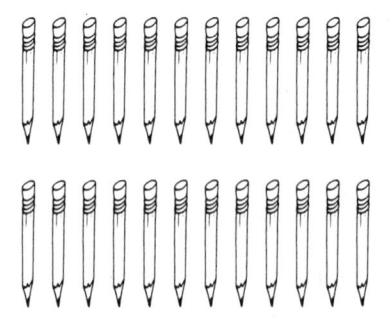

   How many pencils would be in 6 full boxes?

   A 30
   B 120
   C 134
   D 144

(3.1A; 3.1B)

5. A classroom has 14 desks. Each desk has 4 legs. A worker replaces all of the desk legs. How many legs did the worker replace?

   Record your answer in the boxes. Then fill in the bubbles. Be sure to use the correct place value.

Reporting Category 2
Computations and Algebraic Relationships

Exercise 20

3.4G: Use strategies and algorithms, including the standard algorithm, to multiply a two-digit number by a one-digit number. Strategies may include mental math, partial products, and the commutative, associative, and distributive properties (Supporting Standard)

(3.1A; 3.1B)

1. Brittany read 3 pages of her library book every day for 1 week. How many pages did she read by the end of the week?

   A 3
   B 7
   C 10
   D 21

(3.1A; 3.1B)

2. Chase folded 76 flyers for the food drive. His brother and sister each folded the same number of flyers. How many flyers did they fold in all?

   A 79
   B 152
   C 218
   D 228

(3.1A; 3.1B; 3.1F)

3. Shane has a scrapbook of football cards. He put 6 cards on each page. The scrapbook has 12 pages. How many football cards does Shane have?

   A 62
   B 66
   C 72
   D 76

(3.1A; 3.1B; 3.1F)

4. There are 15 girls and 14 boys in Mrs. Scott's class. Mrs. Scott wants to give each student 5 pencils. How many pencils will Mrs. Scott need?

   A 15 + 5 = 20
   B 15 × 5 = 75
   C (15 × 5) + 14 = 89
   D (15 + 14) × 5 = 145

(3.1A; 3.1B)

5. Some students are putting gumdrops on cupcakes. They are making 12 cupcakes. Each cupcake will have 2 red gumdrops, 2 green gumdrops, and 3 purple gumdrops.

   How many gumdrops will the students need in all?

   A 84
   B 36
   C 24
   D 12

Reporting Category 2
Computations and Algebraic Relationships

Exercise 21

3.4G: Use strategies and algorithms, including the standard algorithm, to multiply a two-digit number by a one-digit number. Strategies may include mental math, partial products, and the commutative, associative, and distributive properties (Supporting Standard)

(3.1A; 3.1B)

1. Jenny bought 4 packages of balloons for a party. If there were 24 balloons in each package, how many balloons did Jenny buy in all?

   A 28
   B 72
   C 86
   D 96

(3.1A; 3.1B)

2. Each student in a writing class needs 3 pencils. If there are 32 students in the writing class, what is the total number of pencils they will all need?

   A 35
   B 64
   C 96
   D 99

(3.1A; 3.1B)

3. Harold collects toy cars. He has 7 storage boxes that each hold 16 cars. How many cars can Harold keep in the storage boxes?

   Record your answer in the boxes. Then fill in the bubbles. Be sure to use the correct place value.

(3.1A; 3.1B)

4. Parker, Patrick, and Peter collect baseball cards. If each boy has 56 cards in his collection, how many cards do the three boys have altogether?

   A 59
   B 112
   C 158
   D 168

(3.1A; 3.1B)

5. A school bus travels a route that is 38 miles long. How many miles does the bus travel if it completes the route 4 times?

   Record your answer in the boxes. Then fill in the bubbles. Be sure to use the correct place value.

Reporting Category 2
Computations and Algebraic Relationships

Exercise 22

3.4G: Use strategies and algorithms, including the standard algorithm, to multiply a two-digit number by a one-digit number. Strategies may include mental math, partial products, and the commutative, associative, and distributive properties (Supporting Standard)

(3.1A; 3.1B)

1. Shayla gathers seashells at the beach. She has 9 pails. If she puts 25 seashells into each pail, how many seashells does she have?

   A 34
   B 160
   C 200
   D 225

(3.1A; 3.1B)

2. Harry recorded the number of minutes he read each night for a contest at school. He read 42 minutes each night for 5 nights. How many total minutes did Harry read?

   A 47
   B 200
   C 210
   D 215

(3.1A; 3.1B)

3. Becky rode her bike every day for 5 days. She rode 4 hours each day, and she rode 3 miles every hour. How many miles did Becky ride in all during the 5 days?

   A 15
   B 20
   C 35
   D 60

(3.1A; 3.1B)

4. A teacher made 26 goody bags to use as prizes at a school party. The teacher put 3 small toys and 4 pieces of candy in each bag. What was the total number of items the teacher put in the goody bags?

   Record your answer in the boxes. Then fill in the bubbles. Be sure to use the correct place value.

(3.1A; 3.1B)

5. A school nurse can give hearing tests to 8 students in one hour. Each hearing test lasts about 5 minutes. If the nurse works for 6 hours, how many students could take hearing tests?

   A 40
   B 48
   C 72
   D 240

Reporting Category 2
Computations and Algebraic Relationships

Exercise 23

3.4H: Determine the number of objects in each group when a set of objects is partitioned into equal shares or a set of objects is shared equally (Supporting Standard)

(3.1A; 3.1B; 3.1D)

1. A clown had the balloons shown below.

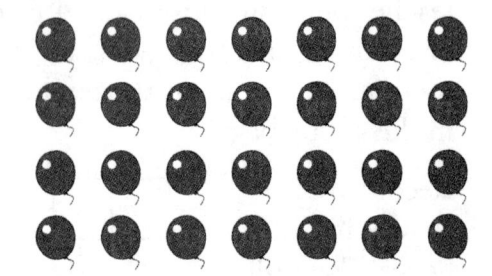

   The clown gave the same number of balloons to each of 7 children. What is the greatest number of balloons the clown could have given to each child?

   A 4
   B 5
   C 7
   D 8

(3.1A; 3.1B; 3.1F)

2. Mrs. Anderson arranged 40 students into groups of 5. How many students were in each group?

   A 6
   B 7
   C 8
   D 10

(3.1A; 3.1B; 3.1D)

3. Jack separated 15 paperclips into 3 equal groups.

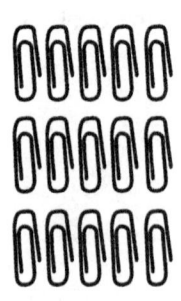

   How many paperclips were in each group?

   A 3
   B 4
   C 5
   D 6

(3.1A; 3.1B; 3.1F)

4. Five art students made 56 table decorations for the cafeteria. If 7 tables will have an equal number of decorations, which number sentence shows the number of decorations on each table?

   A $56 \div 5 = 11$
   B $56 + 7 = 63$
   C $56 - 7 = 49$
   D $56 \div 7 = 8$

Reporting Category 2
Computations and Algebraic Relationships

Exercise 24

3.4H: Determine the number of objects in each group when a set of objects is partitioned into equal shares or a set of objects is shared equally (Supporting Standard)

(3.1A; 3.1B; 3.1D; 3.1F)

1. Look at the diagram below.

   If you separate the balls into groups of 5, which equation shows how many groups you could make?

   A 20 × 5 = 100
   B 20 − 5 = 15
   C 20 ÷ 5 = 4
   D 20 + 5 = 25

(3.1A; 3.1B; 3.1D)

2. Jill had 24 buttons. She sewed 4 buttons on each of her sweaters.

   If Jill used all the buttons, how many sweaters did she have?

   Record your answer in the boxes. Then fill in the bubbles. Be sure to use the correct place value.

(3.1B; 3.1D; 3.1F)

3. Which problem matches the number sentence below?

   15 ÷ 3 = ☐

   A Casey had 15 bows, but lost 3. How many bows did she have left?
   B Casey had 15 bows. How many bows would she have if she bought 3 more?
   C Casey had 3 friends. Each friend had 15 bows. How many bows did the friends have in all?
   D Casey had 15 bows. She gave each of her friends 3 bows. How many friends could receive bows?

(3.1A; 3.1B; 3.1D)

4. Four boys shared 20 slices of pizza equally. How many whole slices of pizza could each boy have?

   A 4
   B 5
   C 6
   D 7

© ECS Learning Systems, Inc.

STAAR MASTER® Student Practice Book—Math, Grade 3

Reporting Category 2
Computations and Algebraic Relationships

Exercise 25

3.4H: Determine the number of objects in each group when a set of objects is partitioned into equal shares or a set of objects is shared equally (Supporting Standard)

(3.1A; 3.1B; 3.1D)

1. Mrs. Marcus gave the oranges shown below to her 6 children.

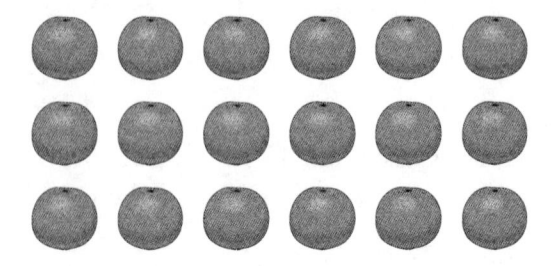

   Mrs. Marcus gave an equal number of oranges to each child. How many oranges did each child receive?

   A 6
   B 4
   C 3
   D 2

(3.1A; 3.1B; 3.1D)

2. Cameron bought the pencils shown below at the store.

   At school, he needs 6 pencils a month. For how many months will Cameron have all the pencils he needs?

   A 5
   B 4
   C 3
   D 2

(3.1A; 3.1B; 3.1D)

3. A teacher has the star stickers shown below to divide equally among 8 students.

   What is the greatest number of stickers each student can receive?

   A 2
   B 3
   C 4
   D 6

(3.1A; 3.1B; 3.1D)

4. Mr. Vu divided the eggs shown below equally among 7 bowls.

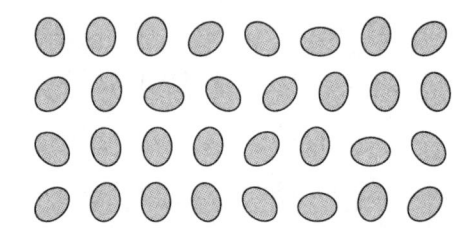

   What is the greatest number of eggs he could place in each bowl?

   A 6
   B 4
   C 3
   D 2

Reporting Category 2
Computations and Algebraic Relationships

Exercise 26

3.4J: Determine a quotient using the relationship between multiplication and division (Supporting Standard)

(3.1F)
1. The numbers 5, 7, and 35 are part of the same family of facts. Which number sentence belongs in this family of facts?

    A 7 − 5 = 2
    B 5 + 7 = 12
    C 35 ÷ 5 = 7
    D 35 − 7 = 28

(3.1F)
2. The diagram below shows the multiplication fact 3 × 6 = 18.

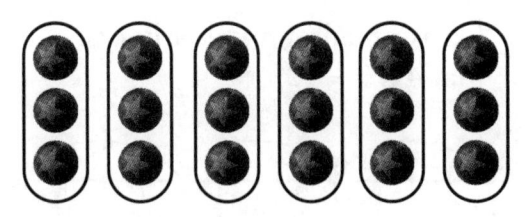

    The diagram also shows that—

    A 3 + 6 = 9
    B 18 ÷ 6 = 3
    C 3 × 7 = 21
    D 18 − 3 = 15

(3.1F)
3. What number is missing from both number sentences below?

    7 × ☐ = 28   28 ÷ 7 = ☐

    A 6
    B 5
    C 4
    D 3

(3.1F)
4. Which number sentence is in the same family of facts as the number sentence below?

    9 × 3 = 27

    A 27 ÷ 3 = 9
    B 9 + 3 = 12
    C 27 × 3 = 81
    D 27 + 3 = 30

Reporting Category 2
Computations and Algebraic Relationships

Exercise 27

3.4J: Determine a quotient using the relationship between multiplication and division (Supporting Standard)

(3.1F)
1. The numbers 7, 9, and 63 are part of the same family of facts. Which number sentence belongs in this family of facts?

   A 9 + 7 = 16
   B 63 ÷ 7 = 9
   C 63 − 7 = 56
   D 63 − 9 = 54

(3.1F)
2. What number is missing from both number sentences below?

   $8 \times \square = 32$ $32 \div 8 = \square$

   A 6
   B 5
   C 4
   D 3

(3.1F)
3. Which number sentence is in the same family of facts as the number sentence below?

   $5 \times 9 = 45$

   A 45 ÷ 9 = 5
   B 5 + 9 = 14
   C 45 − 9 = 36
   D 45 − 5 = 40

(3.1D; 3.1F)
4. Christi made a number line to show that $4 \times 3 = 12$.

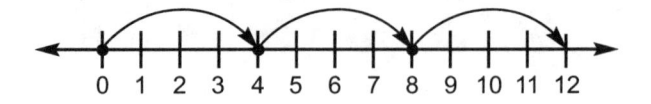

   Christi could use the same arrows and number line to show that—

   A 4 + 3 = 7
   B 12 ÷ 3 = 4
   C 3 × 12 = 36
   D 4 × 12 = 48

Reporting Category 2
Computations and Algebraic Relationships

Exercise 28

3.4J: Determine a quotient using the relationship between multiplication and division (Supporting Standard)

(3.1F)
1. What number is missing from both number sentences below?

    $6 \times \square = 42 \qquad 42 \div 6 = \square$

    A 4
    B 6
    C 7
    D 8

(3.1F)
2. Which number sentence is in the same family of facts as the number sentence below?

    $5 \times \square = 30$

    A $30 \times 5 = \square$
    B $30 - 5 = \square$
    C $30 \div \square = 5$
    D $\square + 5 = 30$

(3.1A; 3.1B)
3. Jake bought the dinner rolls shown below.

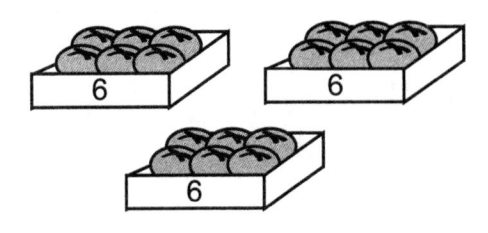

    Jake put 3 rolls on each bread plate. How many bread plates did he use?

    A 2
    B 3
    C 4
    D 6

(3.1A; 3.1B)
4. Julie served 36 cups of punch at a party. She served an equal amount of punch to each of 9 guests. How many cups of punch did Julie serve to each guest?

    A 3
    B 4
    C 6
    D 8

Reporting Category 2
Computations and Algebraic Relationships

Exercise 29

3.4K: Solve one-step and two-step problems involving multiplication and division within 100 using strategies based on objects; pictorial models, including arrays, area models, and equal groups; properties of operations; or recall of facts (Readiness Standard)

(3.1A; 3.1B)

1. Mark bought 3 packages of napkins for a party. Each package held 28 napkins. How many napkins did Mark buy?

   A 31
   B 56
   C 64
   D 84

(3.1A; 3.1B)

2. A trolley travels a route that is 18 miles long. How far does the trolley travel if it completes the route 5 times?

   A 23 miles
   B 50 miles
   C 80 miles
   D 90 miles

(3.1A; 3.1B)

3. Kevin played a game 4 times with his little brother. Kevin won 18 tokens each time he played the game. How many tokens did he win in all?

   Record your answer in the boxes. Then fill in the bubbles. Be sure to use the correct place value.

(3.1A; 3.1B)

4. Mrs. Rashad bought 2 erasers and 3 pencils for each student in her art class. If there were 8 students in the class, how many items did Mrs. Rashad buy for them?

   A 16
   B 24
   C 30
   D 40

(3.1A; 3.1B)

5. Mr. Henry collected 81 magazines for students in his social studies class. He divided the magazines equally among several students. If each student received 9 magazines, how many students received magazines from Mr. Henry?

   A 7
   B 8
   C 9
   D 10

Reporting Category 2
Computations and Algebraic Relationships

Exercise 30

3.4K: Solve one-step and two-step problems involving multiplication and division within 100 using strategies based on objects; pictorial models, including arrays, area models, and equal groups; properties of operations; or recall of facts (Readiness Standard)

(3.1A; 3.1B)

1. A theater gave 72 tickets to a school principal. The principal divided the tickets equally among 3 classes. How many tickets did each class receive?

   A 9
   B 22
   C 24
   D 25

(3.1A; 3.1B)

2. A manager received 96 plums for her store. The plums were packed in 6 boxes, and each box held the same number of plums. How many plums were in each box?

   A 6
   B 11
   C 15
   D 16

(3.1A; 3.1B)

3. Maureen has 6 shells. Her friend Tanya has 3 times as many shells as Maureen. How many shells do the two girls have in all?

   A 9
   B 18
   C 21
   D 24

(3.1A; 3.1B)

4. A bakery normally sells 6 cakes an hour. At that rate, how long would it take the bakery to sell 84 cakes?

   A 8 hours
   B 14 hours
   C 16 hours
   D 18 hours

(3.1A; 3.1B)

5. Dylan had 14 marbles, and his friend Max had 16 marbles. The two boys combined the marbles and then divided them equally among 5 friends. How many marbles did each friend get?

   Record your answer in the boxes. Then fill in the bubbles. Be sure to use the correct place value.

Reporting Category 2
Computations and Algebraic Relationships

Exercise 31

3.4K: Solve one-step and two-step problems involving multiplication and division within 100 using strategies based on objects; pictorial models, including arrays, area models, and equal groups; properties of operations; or recall of facts (Readiness Standard)

(3.1A; 3.1B)

1. Each member of the Martin family used 8 subway tokens while visiting New York City. The family used a total of 48 subway tokens. How many members does the Martin family have?

   A 4
   B 6
   C 8
   D 9

(3.1A; 3.1B)

2. Terry had $45 in five-dollar bills. How many five-dollar bills did Terry have?

   A 5
   B 7
   C 8
   D 9

(3.1A; 3.1B)

3. Colby can make 8 paper airplanes in one hour. At that rate, how many paper airplanes could Colby make in 8 hours?

   A 16
   B 24
   C 36
   D 64

(3.1A; 3.1B)

4. Mrs. Garcia spent $85 on candles for her shop. Each candle cost $5. How many candles did Mrs. Garcia buy?

   A 13
   B 15
   C 17
   D 19

(3.1A; 3.1B)

5. On Monday, Maria rode her bike for 2 hours. On Tuesday, she rode her bike for 3 hours. If Maria can ride 3 miles per hour, how many miles did she ride on Monday and Tuesday?

   Record your answer in the boxes. Then fill in the bubbles. Be sure to use the correct place value.

Reporting Category 2
Computations and Algebraic Relationships

Exercise 32

3.4K: Solve one-step and two-step problems involving multiplication and division within 100 using strategies based on objects; pictorial models, including arrays, area models, and equal groups; properties of operations; or recall of facts (Readiness Standard)

(3.1A; 3.1B)

1. Mr. Keith works 5 days each week and 4 hours each day. How many hours would Mr. Keith work in 3 weeks?

   A 12
   B 20
   C 27
   D 60

(3.1A; 3.1B)

2. Last year, Gracie scored 3 goals in each of her soccer games. If she scored a total of 93 goals, in how many soccer games did Gracie play?

   A 30
   B 31
   C 32
   D 33

(3.1A; 3.1B; 3.1D; 3.1E)

3. The chart below shows how many fish 3 boys caught on a fishing trip.

   Fish Caught on Trip

Boy	Number of Fish
Joshua	8
Adam	7
Matthew	9

   If the boys shared all the fish equally, how many fish did each boy get?

   A 3   C 8
   B 7   D 9

(3.1A; 3.1B)

4. Lily, Jenny, and Karen each bought a book. Lily paid $9 for her book. Jenny paid one third of what Lily paid. Karen paid twice what Jenny paid. How much did the three girls pay for the books in all?

   A $12
   B $16
   C $18
   D $27

(3.1A; 3.1B)

5. Timothy has 48 game tokens. If he uses 6 tokens on each game, how many different games can Timothy play?

   A 9
   B 8
   C 7
   D 6

Reporting Category 2
Computations and Algebraic Relationships

Exercise 33

3.5A: Represent one- and two-step problems involving addition and subtraction of whole numbers to 1,000 using pictorial models, number lines, and equations (Readiness Standard)

(3.1A; 3.1B; 3.1D; 3.1F)

1. Margot saved $125, and James saved $75. Which diagram best shows how much more money Margot saved than James?

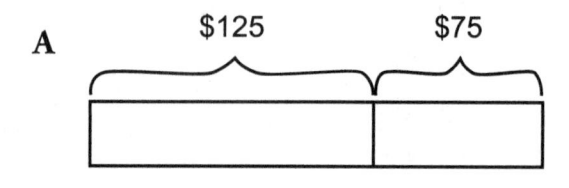

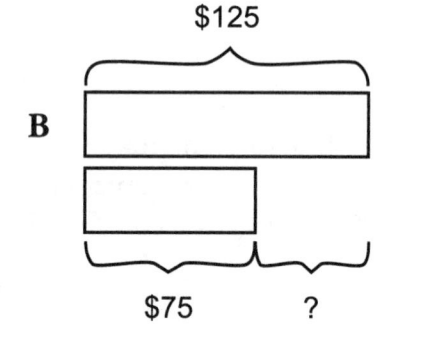

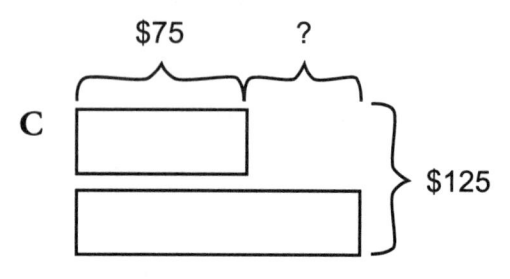

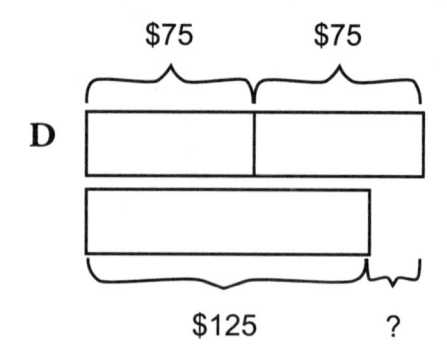

   A [$125 | $75]

   B [$125] / [$75 | ?]

   C [$75 | ?] / [ ] } $125

   D [$75 | $75] / [ ] } $125 ?

(3.1A; 3.1D; 3.1F)

2. In a math game, each color on a cube has a different value.

   ■ = 100   ▨ = 10   □ = 1

   Jane rolls the following during a game.

   ■ ■ ▨ ▨ □ □ □

   What is the value of Jane's roll?

   A 7
   B 23
   C 205
   D 223

(3.1A; 3.1B; 3.1D; 3.1F)

3. At the beginning of the year, School A had 436 students and School B had 395 students. By the end of the year, each school had 20 more students. Which equation can be used to find the total number of students at both schools at the end of the year?

   A 436 + 395 + 20 = ☐
   B 436 + 395 − 20 = ☐
   C 436 − 395 + 20 + 20 = ☐
   D (436 + 20) + (395 + 20) = ☐

Reporting Category 2
Computations and Algebraic Relationships

Exercise 34

3.5A: Represent one- and two-step problems involving addition and subtraction of whole numbers to 1,000 using pictorial models, number lines, and equations (Readiness Standard)

(3.1A; 3.1B; 3.1D; 3.1F)

1. A store had 4 boxes of soap, and each box contained 40 bars of soap. Which diagram best shows how many bars of soap the store would have left if it sold 2 boxes of the soap?

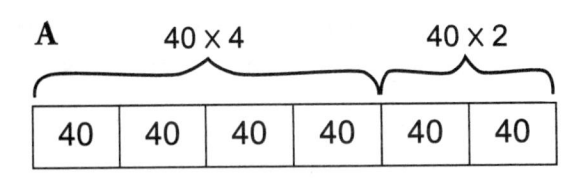

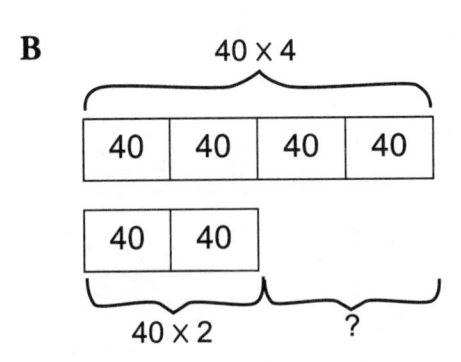

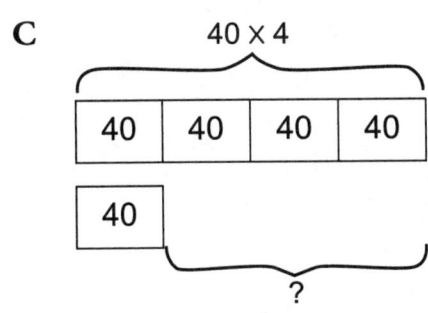

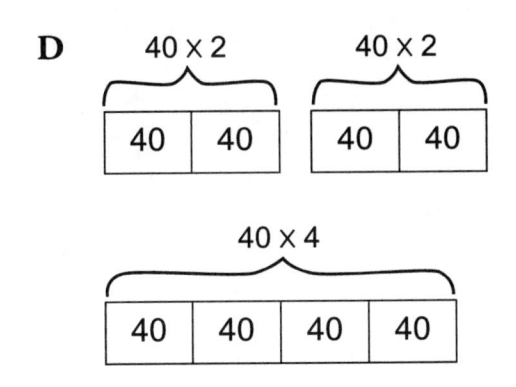

   A 40 × 4 | 40 × 2
   [40 | 40 | 40 | 40 | 40 | 40]

   B 40 × 4
   [40 | 40 | 40 | 40]
   [40 | 40]
   40 × 2   ?

   C 40 × 4
   [40 | 40 | 40 | 40]
   [40]
   ?

   D 40 × 2   40 × 2
   [40 | 40] [40 | 40]
   40 × 4
   [40 | 40 | 40 | 40]

(3.1D; 3.1F)

2. The number line below represents a math problem.

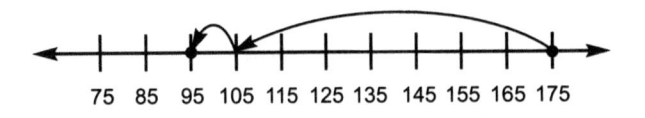

   [number line from 75 to 175 by 10s, with arrows]

   Which equation best represents the same math problem as the number line?

   A 175 − 70 + 10 = ☐
   B 175 − 70 − 10 = ☐
   C (175 + 70) − 10 = ☐
   D 175 + (70 + 10) = ☐

(3.1A; 3.1B; 3.1D; 3.1F)

3. A family saved $965 for a beach vacation. The family spent $280 on a hotel room and $190 on gasoline. Which equation can be used to find how much money the family had left after paying for the hotel room and gasoline?

   A 965 + (280 + 190) = ☐
   B (965 + 280) − 190 = ☐
   C 965 − (280 + 190) = ☐
   D (965 + 190) − 280 = ☐

Reporting Category 2
Computations and Algebraic Relationships

Exercise 35

3.5A: Represent one- and two-step problems involving addition and subtraction of whole numbers to 1,000 using pictorial models, number lines, and equations (Readiness Standard)

(3.1A; 3.1B; 3.1E; 3.1F)

1. The chart below shows the number of pens packed in one box, one carton, and one case.

Pens

Container	Number of Pens
Box	10
Carton	50
Case	150

Mrs. Johnson ordered 2 boxes and 1 case of pens. Which expression can be used to find the total number of pens she ordered?

A 10 + 50 + 150 = ☐

B (10 + 10) + 150 = ☐

C 10 + (150 + 150) = ☐

D (50 + 50) + 150 = ☐

(3.1A; 3.1D; 3.1F)

2. Marta earned $45 for cleaning her grandma's house. She earned $15 for delivering groceries and $25 for babysitting. Which number line best shows the total amount Marta earned?

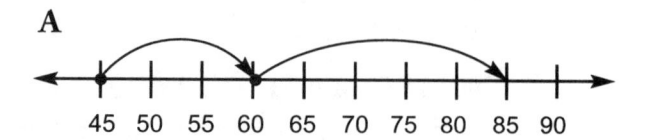

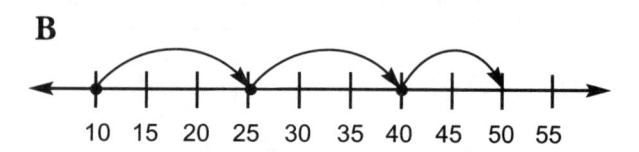

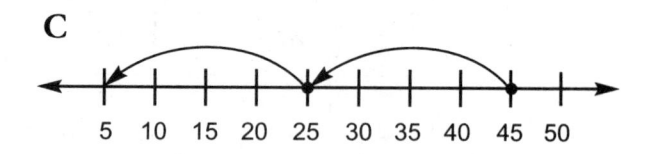

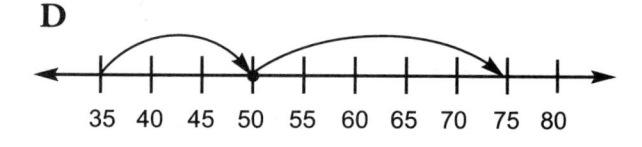

A

45 50 55 60 65 70 75 80 85 90

B

10 15 20 25 30 35 40 45 50 55

C

5 10 15 20 25 30 35 40 45 50

D

35 40 45 50 55 60 65 70 75 80

Reporting Category 2
Computations and Algebraic Relationships

Exercise 36

3.5A: Represent one- and two-step problems involving addition and subtraction of whole numbers to 1,000 using pictorial models, number lines, and equations (Readiness Standard)

(3.1A; 3.1B; 3.1D; 3.1F)

1. Miles is 15 years old, and Jimmy is 8 years older than Miles. Kyle is 4 years younger than Jimmy. Which equation can be used to find Kyle's age?

   A 15 + 8 + 4 = ☐
   B (15 + 8) – 4 = ☐
   C 15 – (8 – 4) = ☐
   D 15 – 8 – 4 = ☐

(3.1A; 3.1B; 3.1D; 3.1F)

2. Mr. Parker drove from his home to his parents' home. He drove 150 miles after breakfast and 125 miles after lunch. After stopping for a snack, he drove the last 55 miles to his parents' home. Which equation can be used to find the total distance Mr. Parker drove?

   A (150 + 125) – 55 = ☐
   B 150 + 125 + 55 = ☐
   C (125 + 55) – 150 = ☐
   D (150 – 125) + 55 = ☐

(3.1A; 3.1B; 3.1D; 3.1F; 3.1G)

3. Which word problem best represents the strip diagram below?

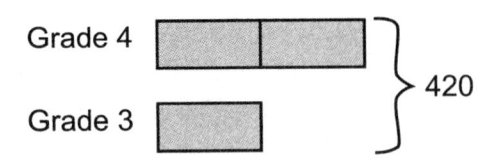

   Grade 4 [☐ | ☐]
   Grade 3 [☐]   } 420

   A Students in Grade 4 sold 420 plants to raise money for their school. Students in Grade 3 sold half that number of plants. How many plants did students in Grade 3 sell?

   B Students in Grade 4 sold 420 plants to raise money for their school. Students in Grade 3 sold the same number of plants. How many plants did the students in Grades 3 and 4 sell in all?

   C Students in Grades 3 and 4 sold a total of 420 plants to raise money for their school. Students in Grade 4 sold twice as many plants as students in Grade 3. How many plants did each grade sell?

   D Students in Grades 3 and 4 sold a total of 420 plants to raise money for their school. Students in Grade 4 sold three times as many plants as students in Grade 3. How many plants did each grade sell?

Reporting Category 2
Computations and Algebraic Relationships

Exercise 37

3.5A: Represent one- and two-step problems involving addition and subtraction of whole numbers to 1,000 using pictorial models, number lines, and equations (Readiness Standard)

(3.1A; 3.1D; 3.1F)

1. In September, an elementary school had 875 students. By December, the school had 50 fewer students than in September. Which number line best shows the total number of students at the school in December?

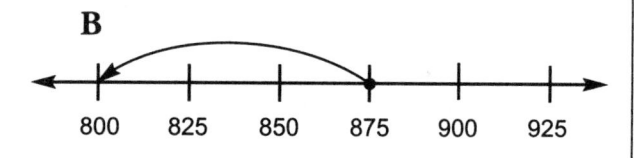

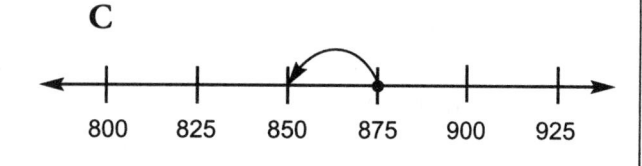

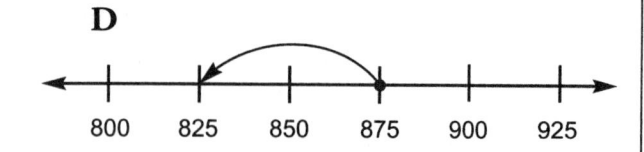

   A

   800 825 850 875 900 925

   B

   800 825 850 875 900 925

   C

   800 825 850 875 900 925

   D

   800 825 850 875 900 925

(3.1A; 3.1B; 3.1D; 3.1F)

2. Justin had 620 tokens to spend at Pizza Palace. He bought a kite for 180 tokens and a toy car for 250 tokens. Which equation can be used to find how many tokens Justin had left after buying both items?

   A $(180 + 250) - 620 = \square$
   B $620 + (250 - 180) = \square$
   C $620 - (180 + 250) = \square$
   D $180 + 250 + 620 = \square$

(3.1A; 3.1B; 3.1D; 3.1F)

3. Recess time for third-grade students is usually 15 minutes. Last week, the third-grade teachers added 5 extra minutes for recess on Monday and Tuesday. Which equation can be used to find how many minutes of reccess third-grade students had in all on Monday and Tuesday?

   A $15 + 5 + 5 = \square$
   B $(15 + 5) + (15 + 5) = \square$
   C $(15 + 5) - (5 + 5) = \square$
   D $(15 + 15 + 15) + (5 + 5) = \square$

Reporting Category 2
Computations and Algebraic Relationships

Exercise 38

3.5A: Represent one- and two-step problems involving addition and subtraction of whole numbers to 1,000 using pictorial models, number lines, and equations (Readiness Standard)

(3.1A; 3.1D; 3.1F)

1. On Monday, a bakery had 332 cookies to sell. By the end of the day, the bakery had sold 114 cookies. In which model does the shaded portion represent the number of cookies the bakery had left to sell after Monday?

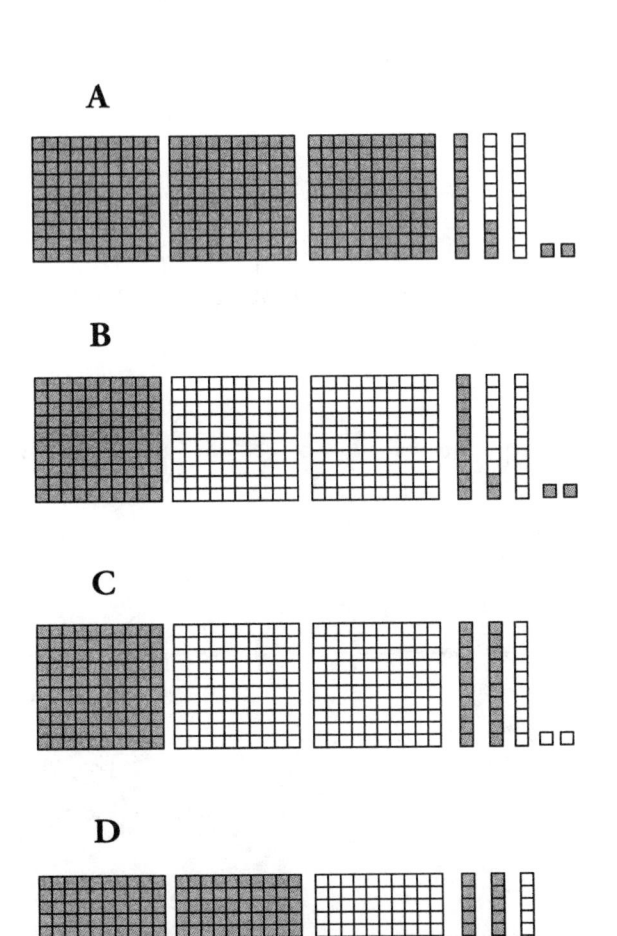

   A

   B

   C

   D

(3.1A; 3.1B; 3.1D; 3.1F; 3.1G)

2. Which word problem best represents the strip diagram below?

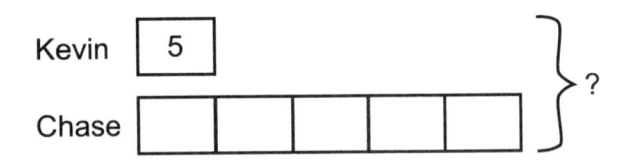

   Kevin [5]
   Chase [ ][ ][ ][ ][ ] } ?

   A Kevin sold 5 school raffle tickets. Chase sold 10 raffle tickets. How many raffle tickets did the two boys sell in all?

   B Kevin sold 5 school raffle tickets. Chase sold 4 more raffle tickets than Kevin. How many raffle tickets did the two boys sell in all?

   C Kevin sold 5 school raffle tickets. Chase sold 5 times as many raffle tickets as Kevin. How many raffle tickets did the two boys sell in all?

   D Kevin sold 5 school raffle tickets. Chase sold 10 times as many raffle tickets as Kevin. How many raffle tickets did the two boys sell in all?

Reporting Category 2
Computations and Algebraic Relationships

Exercise 39

3.5A: Represent one- and two-step problems involving addition and subtraction of whole numbers to 1,000 using pictorial models, number lines, and equations (Readiness Standard)

(3.1A; 3.1B; 3.1D)

1. In math class, 6 students each made a pentagon like the one shown below.

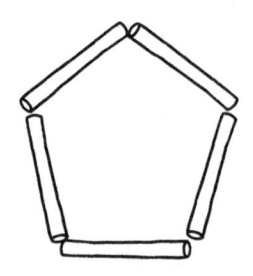

   What was the total number of straws the students used to make all the pentagons?

   A 10
   B 11
   C 24
   D 30

(3.1A; 3.1B; 3.1D; 3.1F)

2. Dorothy wants to make 5 paper flowers like the one shown below. Each flower will have 4 petals.

   Which equation can Dorothy use to find the number of petals she will need for all 5 flowers?

   A $5 + 4 = \square$
   B $5 + 5 + 4 + 4 = \square$
   C $4 + 4 + 4 + 4 + 4 = \square$
   D $5 + 5 + 5 + 5 + 5 = \square$

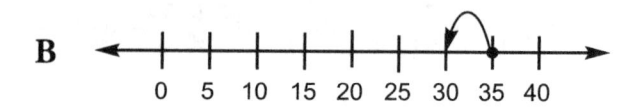

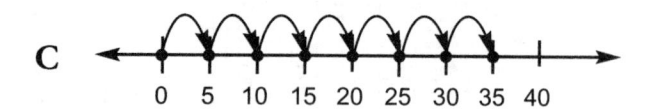

(3.1A; 3.1D; 3.1F)

3. Darius has 35¢ to buy new pencils at the school store. Each new pencil costs 5¢. Which number line shows how many pencils Darius can buy with his money?

   A (number line 0 to 40 by 5s, arc from 35 to 5)

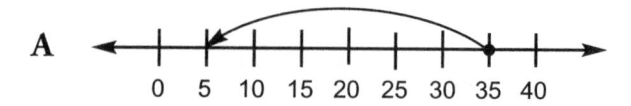

   B (number line 0 to 40 by 5s, arc from 35 to 30)

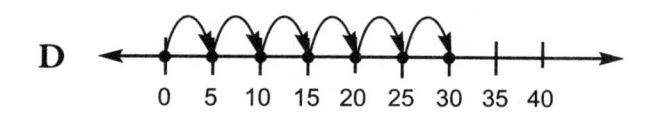

   C (number line 0 to 40 by 5s, arrows from 0 to 5 to 10 to 15 to 20 to 25 to 30 to 35)

   D (number line 0 to 40 by 5s, arrows from 0 to 5 to 10 to 15 to 20 to 25 to 30)

Reporting Category 2
Computations and Algebraic Relationships

Exercise 40

3.5B: Represent and solve one- and two-step multiplication and division problems within 100 using arrays, strip diagrams, and equations (Readiness Standard)

(3.1A; 3.1D; 3.1F)

1. A store sells gift baskets. Each basket includes 2 apples and 3 oranges. Last week, the store sold 6 gift baskets. Which array shows how many pieces of fruit were used in the baskets?

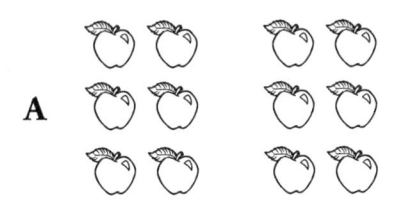

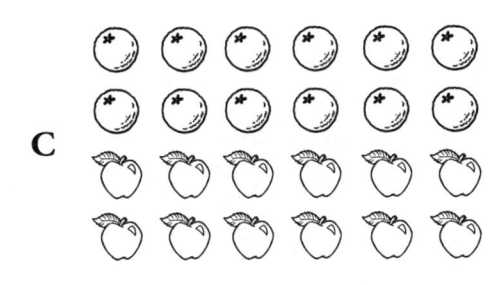

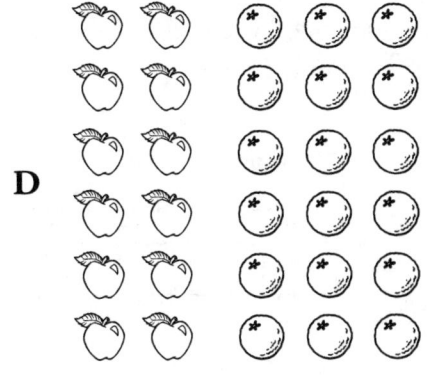

    A
    B
    C
    D

(3.1A; 3.1B; 3.1D; 3.1F)

2. At a factory, a worker packs 18 notebooks into each box. According to the diagram below, how many notebooks would the worker need to pack 6 boxes?

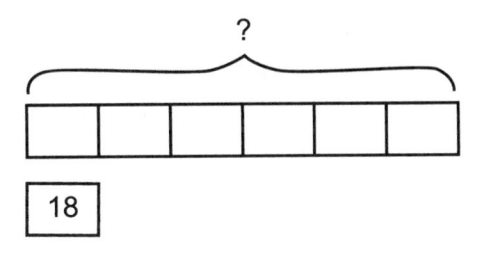

    A 90
    B 100
    C 108
    D 126

(3.1A; 3.1B; 3.1D; 3.1F)

3. A store sells tennis balls in boxes of 5. On Monday, the store sold 8 boxes of tennis balls. On Tuesday, the store sold 9 boxes of tennis balls. Which equation could you use to find the total number of tennis balls the store sold on Monday and Tuesday?

    A $5 \times 8 \times 9 = \square$
    B $5 + 8 + 9 = \square$
    C $(8 \times 9) + 5 = \square$
    D $5 \times (8 + 9) = \square$

Reporting Category 2
Computations and Algebraic Relationships

Exercise 41

3.5B: Represent and solve one- and two-step multiplication and division problems within 100 using arrays, strip diagrams, and equations (Readiness Standard)

(3.1A; 3.1B; 3.1D; 3.1F)

1. A bakery sells cupcakes in boxes of 12.

   | 12 |

   On Monday, the bakery sold 2 boxes of cupcakes before lunch and 4 boxes of cupcakes after lunch. Which diagram best represents the total number of cupcakes the bakery sold on Monday?

   A | 12 | 12 |

   B | 12 | 12 | 12 | 12 |

   C | 12 | 12 | 12 | 12 | 12 |

   D | 12 | 12 | 12 | 12 | 12 | 12 |

(3.1A; 3.1B; 3.1D)

2. Logan walked 40 meters from his house to the soccer field in 8 minutes. He walked at a steady pace. Which equation shows how to find about how far Logan walked in 1 minute?

   A 40 + 8 = ☐
   B 8 + ☐ = 40
   C 8 × ☐ = 40
   D 40 × 8 = ☐

(3.1A; 3.1B; 3.1D; 3.1F)

3. Darla raises chickens and ducks. She has 96 chickens, which is 6 times the number of ducks she has. How many ducks does Darla have?

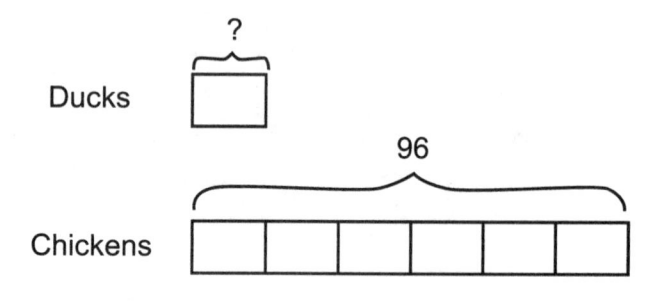

   A 15
   B 16
   C 90
   D 102

(3.1A; 3.1B; 3.1D; 3.1F)

4. Margie has saved $24.

   She will need 6 times that amount to buy a new bicycle.

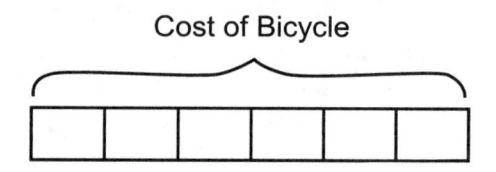

   How much money does Margie need to buy a new bicycle?

   A $4   **C** $124
   B $30   **D** $144

Reporting Category 2
Computations and Algebraic Relationships

Exercise 42

3.5B: Represent and solve one- and two-step multiplication and division problems within 100 using arrays, strip diagrams, and equations (Readiness Standard)

(3.1A; 3.1B; 3.1D)

1. Reggie has 90 baseball cards to put into display binders. Each page holds 6 cards. Which equation correctly shows how many pages Reggie will need for all his cards?

   A $6 \times 6 = 36$
   B $84 \div 6 = 14$
   C $90 \times 6 = 540$
   D $90 \div 6 = 15$

(3.1A; 3.1B; 3.1D)

2. A cake recipe calls for 3 cups of flour and 1 cup of sugar. A chef wants to make 12 of the cakes. Which equation shows how many cups of flour and sugar the chef will use to make all the cakes?

   A $1 \times 12 = \square$
   B $3 \times 12 = \square$
   C $12 + 3 + 1 = \square$
   D $12 \times (3 + 1) = \square$

(3.1A; 3.1B; 3.1D)

3. During an elementary-school field trip, 72 students formed 8 lines. An equal number of students were in each line. Which equation correctly shows how many students were in each line?

   A $80 \div 8 = 10$
   B $72 \div 8 = 9$
   C $72 \div 6 = 12$
   D $64 \div 8 = 8$

(3.1A; 3.1B; 3.1D; 3.1F; 3.1G)

4. The diagram below represents a word problem.

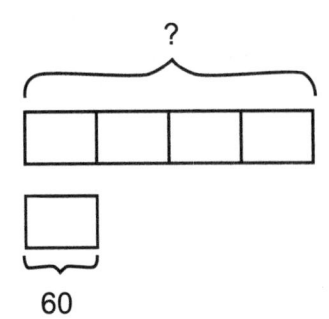

   60

   Which word problem below does the diagram best represent?

   A Karen bought 4 boxes of small beads. Each box contained 60 beads. How many small beads did Karen buy in all?

   B Karen bought 4 boxes of small beads. Her friend Ella bought 3 boxes of small beads. How many beads did the two girls buy in all?

   C Karen bought 1 box of small beads. Her friend Ella bought 3 boxes of small beads. How many more small beads did Ella buy than Karen?

   D Karen and Ella each bought 1 box of small beads. Karen's box had more beads than Ella's box. How many beads did the two girls buy in all?

Reporting Category 2
Computations and Algebraic Relationships

Exercise 43

3.5B: Represent and solve one- and two-step multiplication and division problems within 100 using arrays, strip diagrams, and equations (Readiness Standard)

(3.1A; 3.1B; 3.1D; 3.1F)

1. A principal displayed 48 student pictures in rows on a bulletin board. Each row of pictures had 8 individual student pictures. Which array correctly shows how the pictures appeared on the bulletin board?

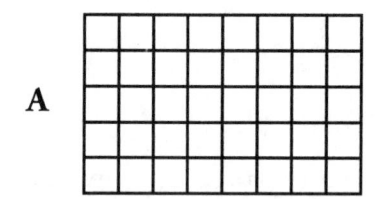

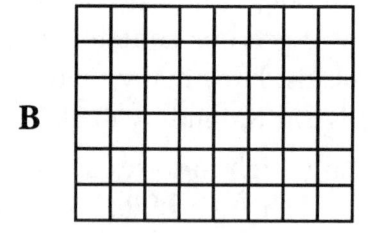

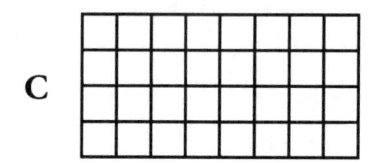

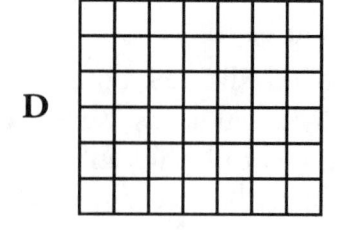

   A

   B

   C

   D

(3.1A; 3.1B; 3.1D; 3.1F)

2. For a party, a florist placed a total of 220 roses in vases. The florist placed 8 roses in each vase. Which equation could you use to find the number of vases the florist used?

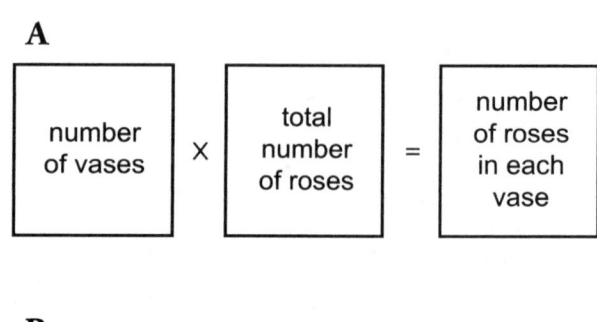

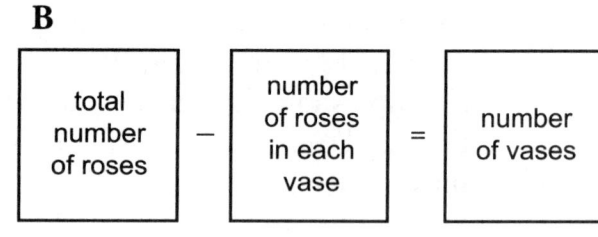

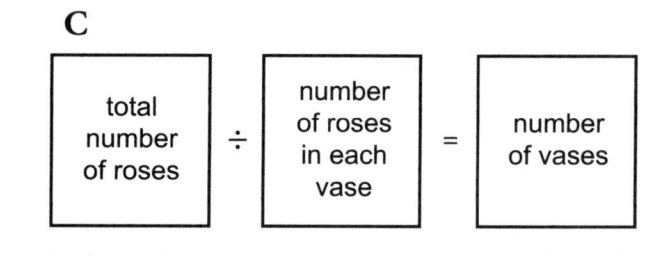

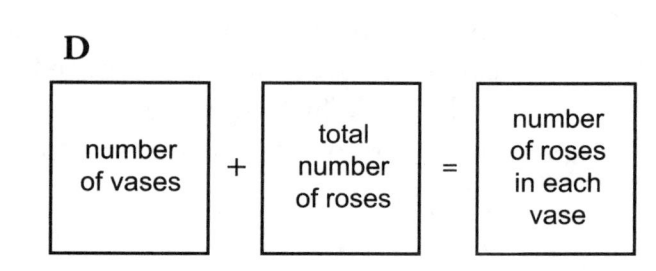

   A
   [number of vases] × [total number of roses] = [number of roses in each vase]

   B
   [total number of roses] − [number of roses in each vase] = [number of vases]

   C
   [total number of roses] ÷ [number of roses in each vase] = [number of vases]

   D
   [number of vases] + [total number of roses] = [number of roses in each vase]

Reporting Category 2
Computations and Algebraic Relationships

Exercise 44

3.5C: Describe a multiplication expression as a comparison such as 3 x 24 represents 3 times as much as 24 (Supporting Standard)

(3.1A; 3.1B)

1. Therese has 4 times as many blocks as her brother Mike. If Mike has 8 blocks, how many blocks does Therese have?

   A 2
   B 12
   C 32
   D 36

(3.1A; 3.1B)

2. Kelly has two dogs, Max and Bumper. Max weighs 30 pounds, which is 5 times as much as Bumper weighs. How much does Bumper weigh?

   A 5 lb
   B 6 lb
   C 35 lb
   D 150 lb

(3.1A; 3.1B)

3. In April, a school club raised $84 at a bake sale. In May, the same club raised 3 times as much money at another bake sale. How much money did the club earn at the bake sale in May?

   A $28
   B $87
   C $242
   D $252

Use the chart below to answer questions 4 and 5.

Lengths of Boats

Name of Boat	Length (ft)
Athena	40
Chugger	18
Sail Along	27
Little Lady	36
The Falcon	10

(3.1A; 3.1B; 3.1E; 3.1G)

4. Which statement correctly compares the lengths of *Chugger* and *Little Lady*?

   A *Little Lady* is twice as long as *Chugger*.
   B *Chugger* is twice as long as *Little Lady*.
   C *Little Lady* is 3 times as long as *Chugger*.
   D *Chugger* is 8 feet shorter than *Little Lady*.

(3.1A; 3.1B; 3.1E)

5. *Athena* is 4 times as long as—

   A *Chugger*
   B *Little Lady*
   C *Sail Along*
   D *The Falcon*

Reporting Category 2
Computations and Algebraic Relationships

Exercise 45

3.5C: Describe a multiplication expression as a comparison such as 3 x 24 represents 3 times as much as 24 (Supporting Standard)

(3.1A; 3.1B)

1. Brenda's bedroom is 12 feet long. Her home is 5 times as long as her bedroom. How long is Brenda's home?

   A   7 ft
   B   17 ft
   C   50 ft
   D   60 ft

(3.1A; 3.1B; 3.1D; 3.1F)

2. Mr. Luna is 4 times older than his son Mitch. Which expression shows how to find Mitch's age?

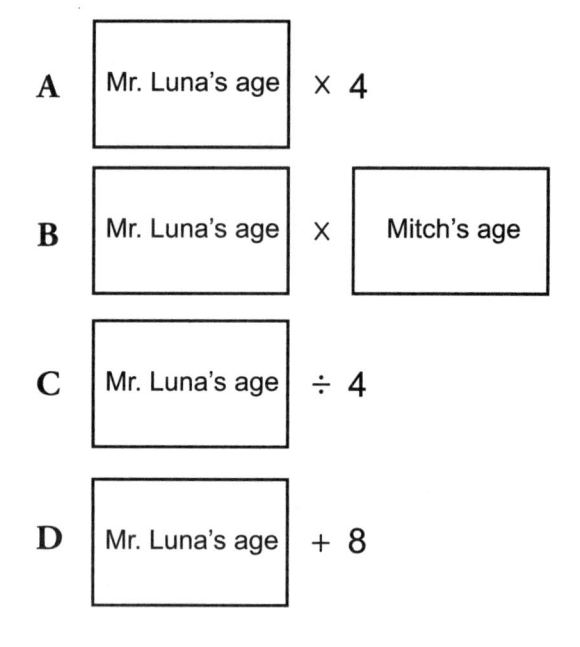

   A | Mr. Luna's age | × 4

   B | Mr. Luna's age | × | Mitch's age |

   C | Mr. Luna's age | ÷ 4

   D | Mr. Luna's age | + 8

(3.1A; 3.1B)

3. Gracie played a computer game and earned 56 points on the first round. On the last round of the game, she earned 8 times as many points as on the first round. How many points did Gracie earn on the last round?

   A   7
   B   64
   C   448
   D   504

(3.1A; 3.1B)

4. A set of new dishes costs $180 at a store. That price is 5 times the price of the same dishes 20 years ago. How much did the dishes cost 20 years ago?

   A $36
   B $56
   C $185
   D $900

(3.1A; 3.1B)

5. Donna's dog weighs 3 times as much as Dylan's dog. If Dylan's dog weighs 27 pounds, how much does Donna's dog weigh?

   A   9 lb
   B   30 lb
   C   61 lb
   D   81 lb

Reporting Category 2
Computations and Algebraic Relationships

Exercise 46

3.5C: Describe a multiplication expression as a comparison such as 3 x 24 represents 3 times as much as 24 (Supporting Standard)

The chart below shows the high temperatures in ten U.S. cities on September 30. Use the chart to answer questions 1 and 2.

High Temperatures in Ten U.S. Cities on September 30

City	High Temperature (°F)
Anchorage, AK	20
El Paso, TX	100
Chicago, IL	55
Portland, ME	45
Pensacola, FL	70
New York, NY	50
Los Angeles, CA	80
Baltimore, MD	60
Minot, ND	40
Las Vegas, NV	120

(3.1A; 3.1B; 3.1E)

1. In which city was the high temperature 6 times the high temperature in Anchorage?

   A El Paso
   B Las Vegas
   C Los Angeles
   D Pensacola

(3.1A; 3.1E; 3.1G)

2. Which statement correctly compares the high temperatures in Minot and Los Angeles?

   A The high temperature in Los Angeles was twice the high temperature in Minot.
   B The high temperature in Los Angeles was 4 times the high temperature in Minot.
   C The high temperature in Minot was twice the high temperature in Los Angeles.
   D The high temperature in Los Angeles was 5 times the high temperature in Minot.

(3.1A; 3.1B; 3.1D; 3.1E)

3. A large restaurant has 8 times as many tables as a small café. Which expression shows how to find the number of tables in the large restaurant?

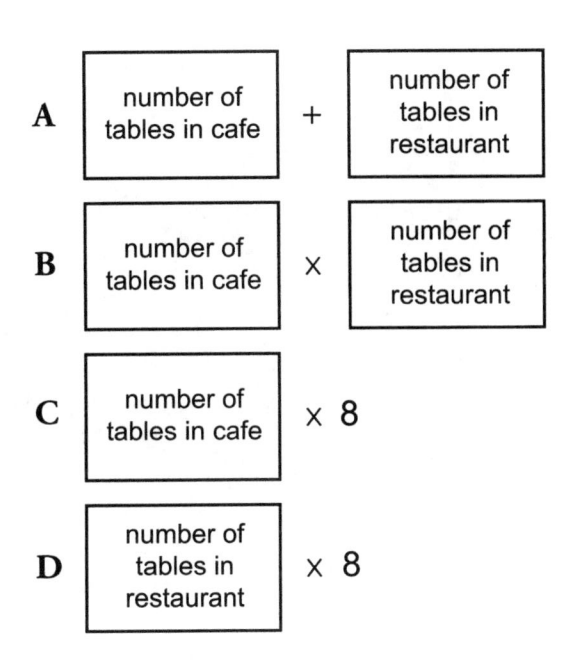

   A [number of tables in cafe] + [number of tables in restaurant]
   B [number of tables in cafe] × [number of tables in restaurant]
   C [number of tables in cafe] × 8
   D [number of tables in restaurant] × 8

Reporting Category 2
Computations and Algebraic Relationships

Exercise 47

3.5D: Determine the unknown whole number in a multiplication or division equation relating three whole numbers when the unknown is either a missing factor or product (Supporting Standard)

(3.1F)
1. The numbers in the triangle below represent two numbers in a fact family.

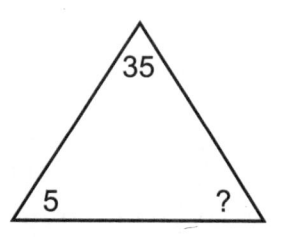

   (triangle with 35 at top, 5 at bottom left, ? at bottom right)

   Which number is part of the same fact family?

   A 6
   B 7
   C 8
   D 9

(3.1F)
2. What number is missing from the equation below?

   $$2 \times \square = 24$$

   A 6
   B 8
   C 10
   D 12

(3.1F)
3. What number is missing from this family of facts?

   $9 \times \square = 27$ $\square \times 9 = 27$
   $27 \div \square = 9$ $27 \div 9 = \square$

   A 2
   B 3
   C 5
   D 18

(3.1A; 3.1F)
4. Henry gave pennies to each of his 7 friends. Each friend received an equal share of 63 pennies. How many pennies did Henry give to each friend?

   $$63 \div 7 = \square$$

   A 6
   B 7
   C 8
   D 9

(3.1A; 3.1F)
5. Cara paid a total of 72¢ for some erasers. Each eraser cost 8¢. How many erasers did Cara buy?

   A 6   C 8
   B 7   D 9

Reporting Category 2
Computations and Algebraic Relationships

Exercise 48

3.5D: Determine the unknown whole number in a multiplication or division equation relating three whole numbers when the unknown is either a missing factor or product (Supporting Standard)

(3.1A; 3.1F)
1. Stephanie placed 32 pennies from her collection in 4 equal rows. How many pennies were in each row?

$$32 \div 4 = \square$$

A 6
B 7
C 8
D 9

(3.1F)
2. The numbers in the triangle below represent two numbers in a fact family.

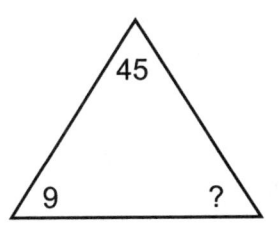

(triangle with 45 at top, 9 at bottom-left, ? at bottom-right)

Which number is part of the same fact family?

A 5
B 6
C 7
D 8

(3.1F)
3. What number is missing from this family of facts?

$$7 \times \square = 28 \qquad \square \times 7 = 28$$
$$28 \div 7 = \square \qquad 28 \div \square = 7$$

A 3
B 4
C 6
D 8

(3.1A; 3.1F)
4. Michelle borrowed 12 library books. At home, she put the same number of library books on each shelf of her bookshelf. If her bookshelf has 4 shelves, how many books did Michelle place on each shelf?

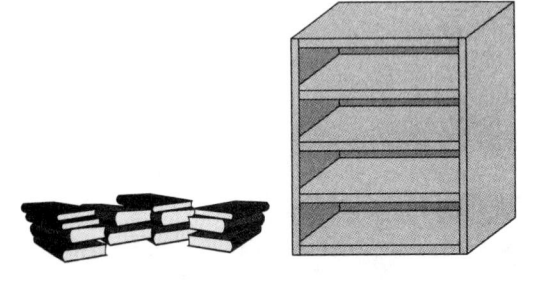

A 3
B 4
C 9
D 16

(3.1A; 3.1F)
5. A school rented vans to take 48 students to the zoo. Eight students could ride in each van. How many vans did the school rent?

$$48 \div \square = 8$$

A 4
B 6
C 8
D 9

Reporting Category 2
Computations and Algebraic Relationships

Exercise 49

3.5D: Determine the unknown whole number in a multiplication or division equation relating three whole numbers when the unknown is either a missing factor or product (Supporting Standard)

(3.1F)
1. Melanie knows that 6 times a number equals 54. To find the missing number, she wrote the following equation.

    $6 \times \square = 54$

    What number is missing from the equation above?

    A 6
    B 8
    C 9
    D 48

(3.1F)
2. Derrick knows that 81 divided by a number equals 9. To find the missing number, he wrote the following equation.

    $81 \div \square = 9$

    What number is missing from the equation above?

    A 6
    B 7
    C 8
    D 9

(3.1F)
3. The numbers on the triangle below represent two numbers in a fact family.

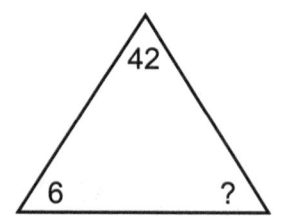

    (triangle with 42 at top, 6 at bottom-left, ? at bottom-right)

    Which number is part of the same fact family?

    A 6
    B 7
    C 8
    D 9

(3.1F)
4. What number is missing from this family of facts?

    $5 \times \square = 40$ $\square \times 5 = 40$
    $40 \div 5 = \square$ $40 \div \square = 5$

    A 5
    B 6
    C 7
    D 8

Reporting Category 2
Computations and Algebraic Relationships

Exercise 50

3.5E: Represent real-world relationships using number pairs in a table and verbal descriptions (Readiness Standard)

(3.1A; 3.1E; 3.1F)

1. The table below shows the number of wheels on different numbers of trucks.

   Wheels on Trucks

Number of Trucks	Number of Wheels
1	4
2	8
3	12
4	16

   Based on the relationship shown in the table, how many wheels would be on 9 trucks?

   A 13   **C** 27
   B 18   **D** 36

(3.1A; 3.1E; 3.1F)

2. A science museum shows several models of triceratops. The table below shows how many horns would appear on different numbers of the models.

   Horns on Triceratops Models

Number of Models	2	4	6	8	10
Number of Horns	6	12	18	24	

   Based on the relationship shown in the table, how many horns would you see on 10 triceratops models?

   A 28   **C** 32
   B 30   **D** 33

(3.1A; 3.1E; 3.1F)

3. Students in an art class made ink handprints on paper. The table shows how many fingers appeared on different numbers of handprints.

   Fingers in Handprints

Number of Handprints	Number of Fingers
3	15
4	20
5	25
6	30

   Based on the relationship shown in the table, how many fingers would appear on 12 handprints?

   A 24   **C** 60
   B 47   **D** 65

(3.1A; 3.1E; 3.1F)

4. A florist places the same number of flowers in each centerpiece for a party. The table below shows how many flowers the florist uses for different numbers of centerpieces.

   Flowers in Centerpieces

Number of Centerpieces	1	2	3	4	5
Number of Flowers	7	14	21	28	35

   Based on the relationship shown in the table, how many flowers will the florist need for 8 centerpieces?

   A 40   **C** 49
   B 43   **D** 56

Reporting Category 2
Computations and Algebraic Relationships

Exercise 51

3.5E: Represent real-world relationships using number pairs in a table and verbal descriptions (Readiness Standard)

(3.1A; 3.1E; 3.1F)

1. A company uses 6 white stripes on each American flag that it makes. Which table correctly shows the number of white stripes the company would need to make 4, 5, and 8 American flags?

A

Flags	White Stripes
4	10
5	11
8	14

B

Flags	White Stripes
4	20
5	30
8	40

C

Flags	White Stripes
4	24
5	30
8	36

D

Flags	White Stripes
4	24
5	30
8	48

(3.1A; 3.1E; 3.1F)

2. Stores sell mittens in pairs. Which table correctly shows the total number of mittens in 9, 11, and 13 pairs?

A

Number of Pairs	9	11	13
Number of Mittens	18	22	26

B

Number of Pairs	9	11	13
Number of Mittens	18	20	22

C

Number of Pairs	9	11	13
Number of Mittens	11	13	15

D

Number of Pairs	9	11	13
Number of Mittens	10	12	14

Reporting Category 2
Computations and Algebraic Relationships

Exercise 52

3.5E: Represent real-world relationships using number pairs in a table and verbal descriptions (Readiness Standard)

(3.1A; 3.1E; 3.1F)

1. The table below shows the total number of pounds a cow gained during a 5-week period of time.

Weight Gained by Cow

Number of Weeks	Total Pounds Gained
1	10
2	20
3	30
4	40
5	50

If the cow continued gaining weight at the same rate shown in the table, how many pounds would the cow have gained after 10 weeks?

A 50
B 80
C 90
D 100

(3.1E; 3.1F)

2. The table below shows related pairs of numbers.

Related Pairs of Numbers

Number A	1	2	3	4	5
Number B	8	16	24	32	40

Based on the relationship shown in the table, which number pair can you use to extend the table?

A 6, 36
B 6, 42
C 6, 48
D 6, 54

(3.1E; 3.1F)

3. The table below shows how many line segments are needed to draw different numbers of pentagons.

Line Segments in Different Numbers of Pentagons

Number of Pentagons	1	3	5	7	9
Number of Line Segments	5	15	25	35	45

Based on the relationship shown in the table, how many line segments would you use to draw 14 pentagons?

A 50
B 55
C 70
D 80

(3.1A; 3.1E; 3.1F)

4. The table below shows how many staples a teacher used to make booklets for his students.

Staples Used for Booklets

Number of Booklets	Number of Staples
1	6
2	12
3	18
4	24

Based on the relationship shown in the table, how many booklets could the teacher make if he used 54 staples?

A 5
B 6
C 8
D 9

Reporting Category 2
Computations and Algebraic Relationships

Exercise 53

3.5E: Represent real-world relationships using number pairs in a table and verbal descriptions (Readiness Standard)

(3.1A; 3.1E; 3.1F)

1. Students in an art class folded square pieces of paper into 4 triangles, as shown below.

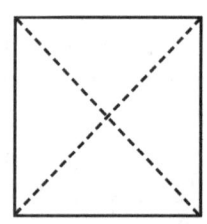

Which table correctly shows the number of triangles each student would have if s/he folded 10, 11, and 13 pieces of paper?

A.

Pieces of Paper	Number of Triangles
10	34
11	38
13	42

B.

Pieces of Paper	Number of Triangles
10	34
11	44
13	54

C.

Pieces of Paper	Number of Triangles
10	40
11	44
13	48

D.

Pieces of Paper	Number of Triangles
10	40
11	44
13	52

(3.1A; 3.1E; 3.1F)

2. Ricky bought T-shirts in packages of 7. Which table correctly shows the total number of T-shirts Ricky will get if he buys 4, 6, or 8 packages of the shirts?

A.

Number of Packages	4	6	8
Number of Shirts	28	42	56

B.

Number of Packages	4	6	8
Number of Shirts	28	35	42

C.

Number of Packages	4	6	8
Number of Shirts	24	36	48

D.

Number of Packages	4	6	8
Number of Shirts	24	30	36

Reporting Category 3
Geometry and Measurement

3.6 A. Classify and sort two- and three-dimensional figures, including cones, cylinders, spheres, triangular and rectangular prisms, and cubes, based on attributes using formal geometric language (Readiness Standard)

B. Use attributes to recognize rhombuses, parallelograms, trapezoids, rectangles, and squares as examples of quadrilaterals, and draw examples of quadrilaterals that do not belong to any of these subcategories (Supporting Standard)

C. Determine the area of rectangles with whole number side lengths in problems using multiplication related to the number of rows times the number of unit squares in each row (Readiness Standard)

D. Decompose composite figures formed by rectangles into non-overlapping rectangles to determine the area of the original figure using the additive property of area (Supporting Standard)

E. Decompose two congruent two-dimensional figures into parts with equal areas and express the area of each part as a unit fraction of the whole, and recognize that equal shares of identical wholes need not have the same shape (Supporting Standard)

3.7 B. Determine the perimeter of a polygon or a missing length when given perimeter and remaining side lengths in problems (Readiness Standard)

C. Determine the solutions to problems involving addition and subtraction of time intervals in minutes using pictorial models or tools such as a 15-minute event plus a 30-minute event equals 45 minutes (Supporting Standard)

D. Determine when it is appropriate to use measurements of liquid volume (capacity) or weight (Supporting Standard)

E. Determine liquid volume (capacity) or weight using appropriate units and tools (Supporting Standard)

Reporting Category 3
Geometry and Measurement

Exercise 1

3.6A: Classify and sort two- and three-dimensional figures, including cones, cylinders, spheres, triangular and rectangular prisms, and cubes, based on attributes using formal geometric language (Readiness Standard)

(3.1F; 3.1G)
1. Look at the objects below.

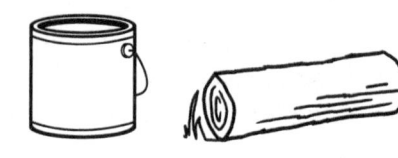

   What attribute do they share?

   A 2 bases
   B 2 vertices
   C 4 angles
   D 4 faces

(3.1F; 3.1G)
2. Look at this teepee made for a class project.

   Which shape does this teepee best represent?

   A Cone
   B Square pyramid
   C Triangle
   D Triangular prism

(3.1F; 3.1G)
3. Carlos used this ball in P.E. class.

   Which shape does a basketball best represent?

   A Circle
   B Cube
   C Cylinder
   D Sphere

(3.1G)
4. Which three-dimensional shape has 5 vertices, 5 faces, and 8 edges?

   A Cube
   B Sphere
   C Square pyramid
   D Triangular prism

Reporting Category 3
Geometry and Measurement

Exercise 2

3.6A: Classify and sort two- and three-dimensional figures, including cones, cylinders, spheres, triangular and rectangular prisms, and cubes, based on attributes using formal geometric language (Readiness Standard)

(3.1F)
1. Look at the drawing below.

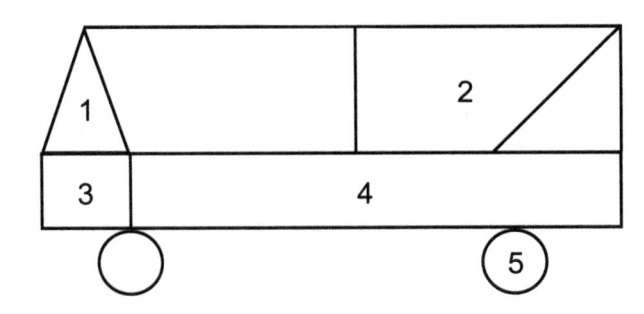

    Which numbered part of the drawing is a triangle?

    A Part 1
    B Part 2
    C Part 3
    D Part 4

(3.1F; 3.1G)
2. Look at figures A and B below.

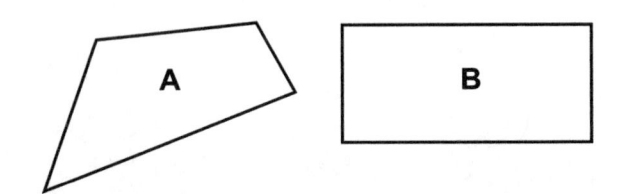

    What name can you use for both figures?

    A Parallelogram
    B Prism
    C Quadrilateral
    D Rectangle

(3.1F)
3. Look at the group of triangles below.

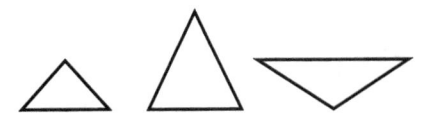

    Which triangle belongs in the group shown above?

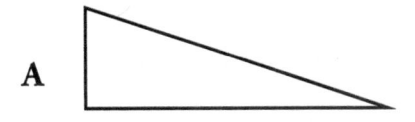

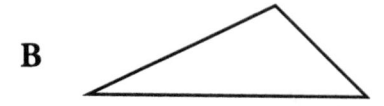

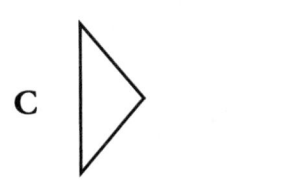

    A
    B
    C
    D

© ECS Learning Systems, Inc.   STAAR MASTER® Student Practice Book—Math, Grade 3   99

Reporting Category 3
Geometry and Measurement

Exercise 3

3.6A: Classify and sort two- and three-dimensional figures, including cones, cylinders, spheres, triangular and rectangular prisms, and cubes, based on attributes using formal geometric language (Readiness Standard)

(3.1F)
1. Look at figures A, B, and C below.

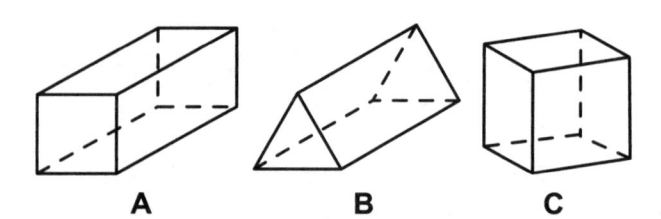

   A   B   C

   Which figure belongs in the group of figures shown above?

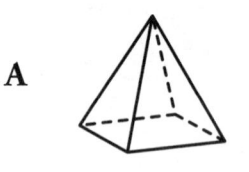

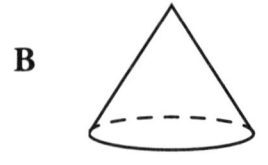

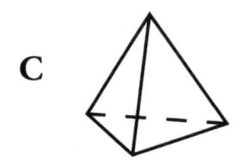

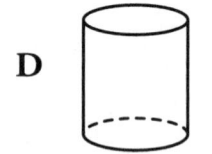

   A

   B

   C

   D

(3.1G)
2. Which figure below has 5 faces, 9 edges, and 6 vertices?

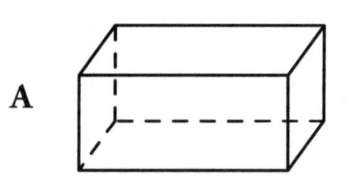

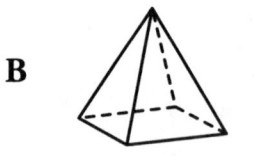

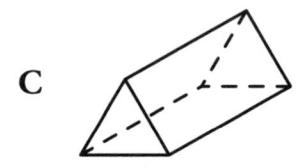

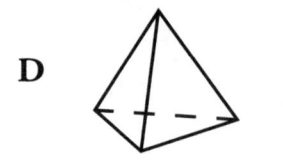

   A

   B

   C

   D

---

100   STAAR MASTER® Student Practice Book—Math, Grade 3   © ECS Learning Systems, Inc.

Reporting Category 3
Geometry and Measurement

Exercise 4

3.6A: Classify and sort two- and three-dimensional figures, including cones, cylinders, spheres, triangular and rectangular prisms, and cubes, based on attributes using formal geometric language (Readiness Standard)

(3.1G)
1. Which figure below has 6 faces and 12 edges?

   A 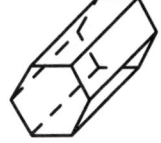
   B 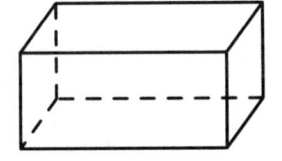
   C 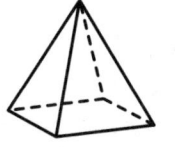
   D

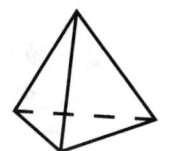

(3.1G)
2. Look at the cube below.

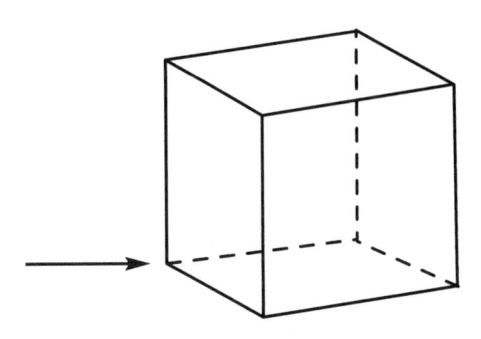

   The arrow points to the cube's—

   A edge
   B face
   C side
   D vertex

(3.1G)
3. How many edges does a rectangular pyramid have?

   A 4
   B 6
   C 8
   D 12

Reporting Category 3
Geometry and Measurement

Exercise 5

3.6A: Classify and sort two- and three-dimensional figures, including cones, cylinders, spheres, triangular and rectangular prisms, and cubes, based on attributes using formal geometric language (Readiness Standard)

(3.1F; 3.1G)

1. Look at the figure below.

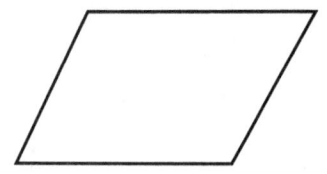

   The figure is both a—

   A trapezoid and a rectangle
   B quadrilateral and a square
   C rectangle and a parallelogram
   D parallelogram and a quadrilateral

(3.1G)

2. Which of the following is a characteristic of all squares?

   A 5 sides
   B 3 equal sides
   C 4 equal sides
   D 2 long sides, 2 short sides

(3.1G)

3. Look at the square pyramid below.

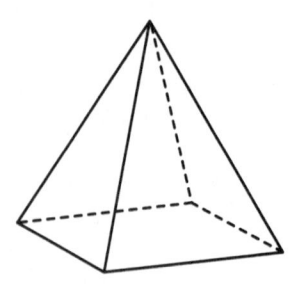

   How many faces does the square pyramid have?

   A 3   C 5
   B 4   D 8

(3.1G)

4. Look at the cube below.

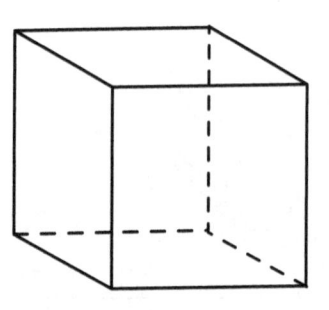

   How many vertices does the cube have?

   A 4
   B 6
   C 8
   D 12

(3.1F; 3.1G)

5. Look at the four figures below.

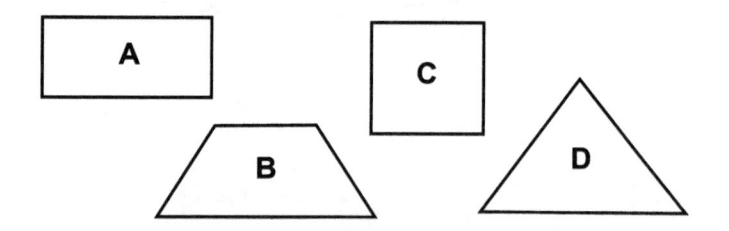

   What name can you use for all four figures in the group?

   A Parallelogram
   B Polygon
   C Quadrilateral
   D Rectangle

Reporting Category 3
Geometry and Measurement

Exercise 6

3.6A: Classify and sort two- and three-dimensional figures, including cones, cylinders, spheres, triangular and rectangular prisms, and cubes, based on attributes using formal geometric language (Readiness Standard)

(3.1G)

1. Look at the rectangle below.

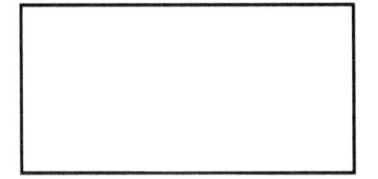

   Which of the following is an attribute of all rectangles?

   A 5 equal sides
   B 8 equal edges
   C 4 equal angles
   D 6 equal angles

(3.1G)

2. Look at the triangle below.

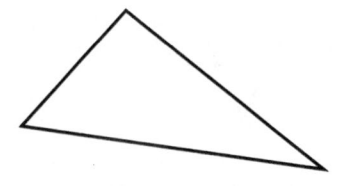

   Which of the following are attributes of all triangles?

   A 3 angles, 3 sides
   B 3 equal angles, 3 equal sides
   C 3 unequal angles, 3 equal sides
   D 3 equal angles, 3 unequal sides

(3.1F; 3.1G)

3. Daniella has these wooden shapes.

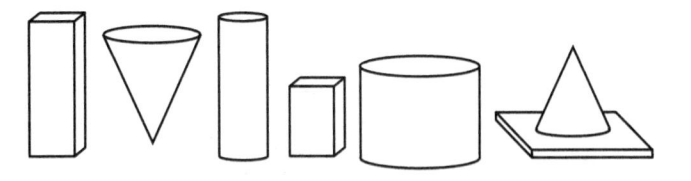

   Which of the following best describes these shapes?

   A Prisms, cylinders, and cones
   B Cubes, pyramids, and cones
   C Rectangles, triangles, and circles
   D Cylinders, spheres, and rectangles

(3.1F; 3.1G)

4. Look at the vase of flowers below.

   What is the shape of the vase?

   A Circle
   B Cone
   C Cube
   D Cylinder

Reporting Category 3
Geometry and Measurement

Exercise 7

3.6B: Use attributes to recognize rhombuses, parallelograms, trapezoids, rectangles, and squares as examples of quadrilaterals, and draw examples of quadrilaterals that do not belong to any of these subcategories (Supporting Standard)

(3.1F; 3.1G)

1. Figure A below is a square.

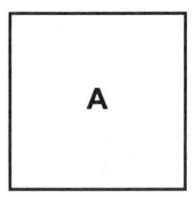

   Figure A is also each of the following **EXCEPT** a—

   A quadrilateral
   B rectangle
   C rhombus
   D trapezoid

(3.1G)

2. Figure B below is a rectangle.

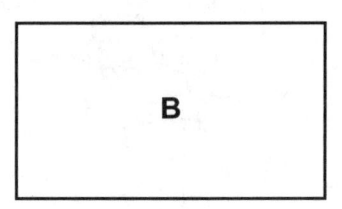

   Which statement about rectangles is false?

   A All rectangles are squares.
   B All rectangles are quadrilaterals.
   C All rectangles are parallelograms.
   D All rectangles have 4 right angles.

(3.1F; 3.1G)

3. Mario drew a group of parallelograms, as shown below.

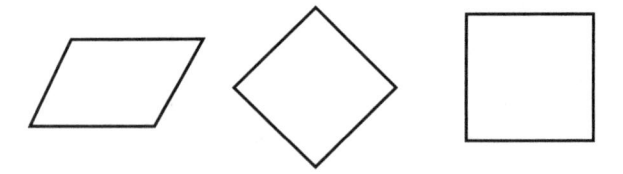

   Mario added one more figure to the group of parallelograms. Which figure could Mario have added?

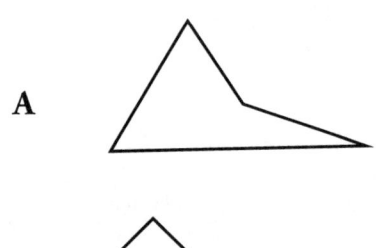

   A
   B
   C 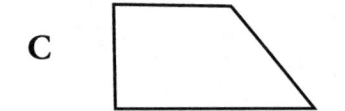
   D

104 STAAR MASTER® Student Practice Book—Math, Grade 3   © ECS Learning Systems, Inc.

Reporting Category 3
Geometry and Measurement

Exercise 8

3.6B: Use attributes to recognize rhombuses, parallelograms, trapezoids, rectangles, and squares as examples of quadrilaterals, and draw examples of quadrilaterals that do not belong to any of these subcategories (Supporting Standard)

(3.1F; 3.1G)

1. Figure C below is a parallelogram.

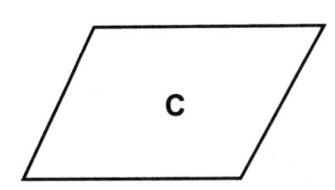

   Each figure below is a parallelogram **EXCEPT**—

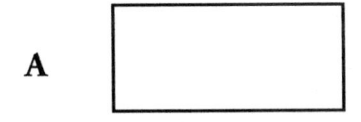

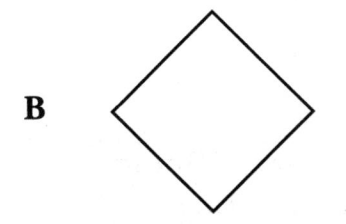

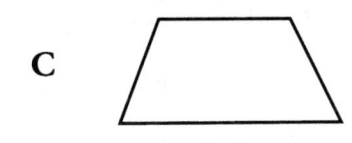

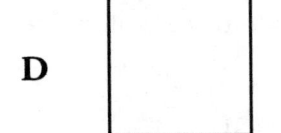

   A
   B
   C
   D

(3.1F; 3.1G)

2. Look at figure A below.

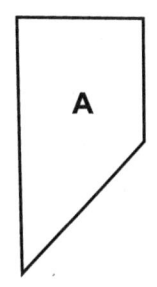

   Which word correctly describes figure A?

   A Parallelogram
   B Quadrilateral
   C Rhombus
   D Square

(3.1F; 3.1G)

3. Anthony drew figures A and B below.

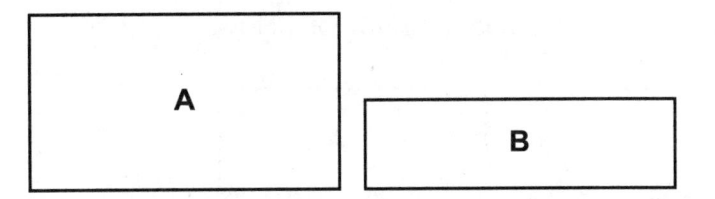

   Which statement about figures A and B is correct?

   A Both figures A and B are rectangles and trapezoids.
   B Both figures A and B are quadrilaterals and squares.
   C Both figures A and B are parallelograms and rectangles.
   D Both figures A and B are parallelograms and rhombuses.

Reporting Category 3
Geometry and Measurement

Exercise 9

3.6B: Use attributes to recognize rhombuses, parallelograms, trapezoids, rectangles, and squares as examples of quadrilaterals, and draw examples of quadrilaterals that do not belong to any of these subcategories (Supporting Standard)

(3.1F; 3.1G)
1. Several figures are shown below.

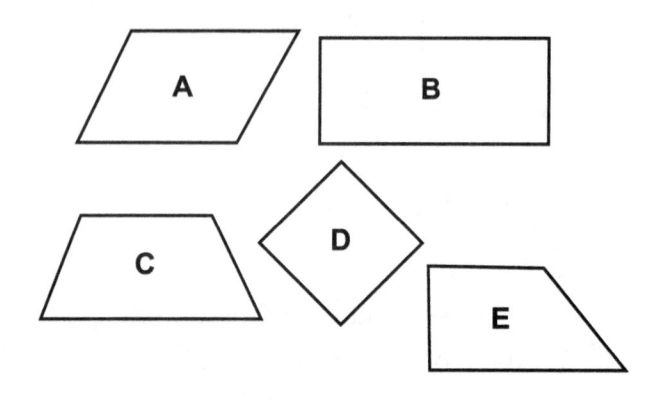

   Which figure above is a rhombus?

   A Figure A
   B Figure C
   C Figure D
   D Figure E

(3.1F; 3.1G)
2. Look at figure A below.

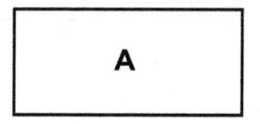

   Figure A is each of the following **EXCEPT** a—

   A parallelogram
   B quadrilateral
   C rectangle
   D square

(3.1F; 3.1G)
3. Look at figure C below.

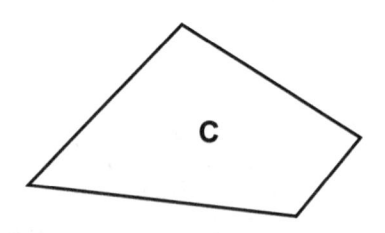

   Figure C is a—

   A parallelogram
   B quadrilateral
   C rhombus
   D square

(3.1F; 3.1G)
4. Figure A below is a square.

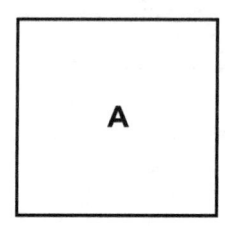

   Figure A is each of the following **EXCEPT** a—

   A parallelogram
   B rectangle
   C rhombus
   D trapezoid

106 STAAR MASTER® Student Practice Book—Math, Grade 3 © ECS Learning Systems, Inc.

Reporting Category 3
Geometry and Measurement

Exercise 10

3.6C: Determine the area of rectangles with whole number side lengths in problems using multiplication related to the number of rows times the number of unit squares in each row (Readiness Standard)

(3.1F)
1. What is the area of the figure below?

   4 in.
   3 in.

   A   4 square inches
   B   7 square inches
   C   10 square inches
   D   12 square inches

(3.1F)
2. What is the area of the figure below?

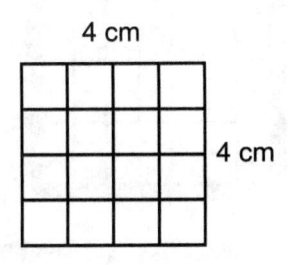

   4 cm
   4 cm

   A   4 square centimeters
   B   12 square centimeters
   C   16 square centimeters
   D   20 square centimeters

(3.1E; 3.1F)
3. Look at the figure below.

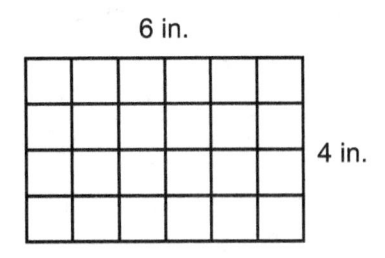

   6 in.
   4 in.

   Which of the following could be added to the figure to make a total area of 40 square inches?

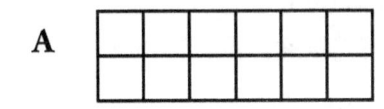

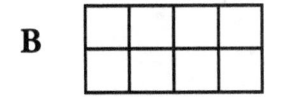

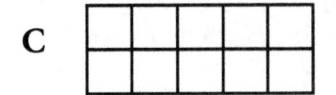

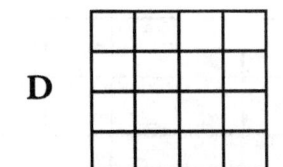

   A
   B
   C
   D

© ECS Learning Systems, Inc.   STAAR MASTER® Student Practice Book—Math, Grade 3   107

Reporting Category 3
Geometry and Measurement

Exercise 11

3.6C: Determine the area of rectangles with whole number side lengths in problems using multiplication related to the number of rows times the number of unit squares in each row (Readiness Standard)

(3.1A; 3.1D; 3.1F)

1. Tiffany plans to make a garden like the one below. What is the area of the whole garden?

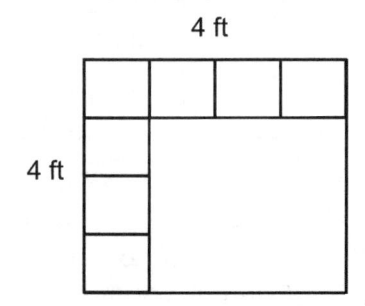

   4 ft
   4 ft

   A 8 square feet
   B 9 square feet
   C 16 square feet
   D 20 square feet

(3.1A; 3.1F)

2. A diagram of a tile floor is shown below. Each tile measures 1 square foot.

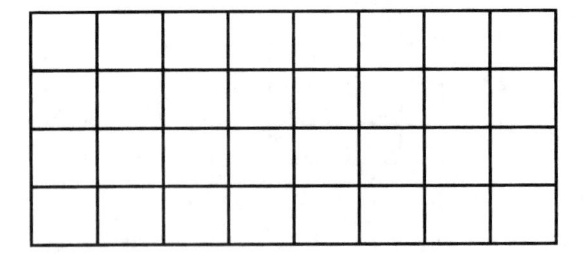

   What is the area of the tile floor?

   A 12 square feet
   B 24 square feet
   C 32 square feet
   D 48 square feet

(3.1A; 3.1E; 3.1F)

3. JoAnn must bake a cake that has an area of 72 square inches. Which pan should she use to bake her cake? (Each pan is marked in square inches.)

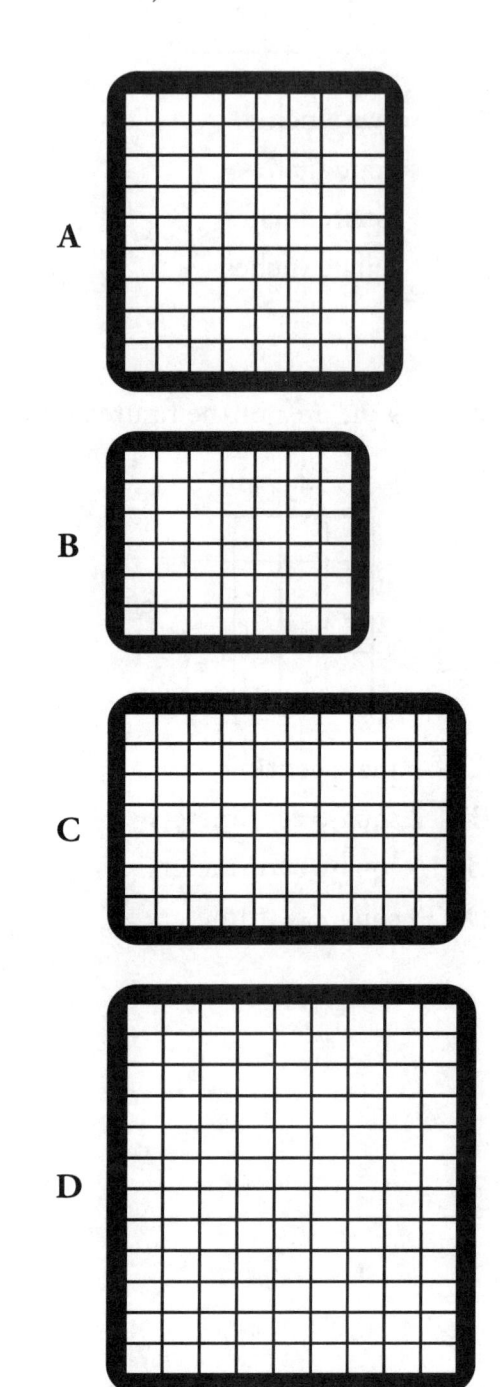

   A

   B

   C

   D

108 STAAR MASTER® Student Practice Book—Math, Grade 3

Reporting Category 3
Geometry and Measurement

Exercise 12

3.6C: Determine the area of rectangles with whole number side lengths in problems using multiplication related to the number of rows times the number of unit squares in each row (Readiness Standard)

(3.1F)
1. What is the area of the diagram below?

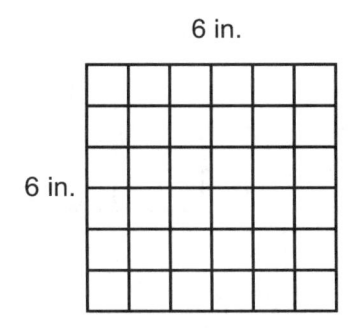

   6 in.
   6 in.

   A 12 square inches
   B 24 square inches
   C 36 square inches
   D 48 square inches

(3.1F)
2. What is the area of the shaded part of the diagram below?

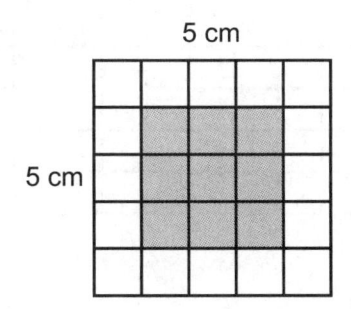

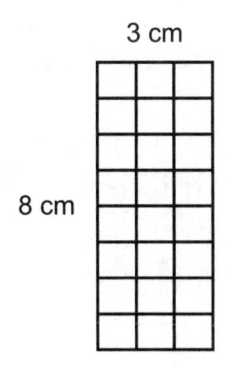

   5 cm
   5 cm

   A 8 square centimeters
   B 9 square centimeters
   C 16 square centimeters
   D 25 square centimeters

(3.1F)
3. What is the area of the diagram below?

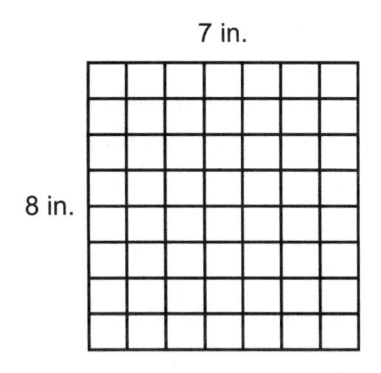

   7 in.
   8 in.

   A 15 square inches
   B 30 square inches
   C 56 square inches
   D 64 square inches

(3.1F)
4. What is the area of the diagram below?

   3 cm
   8 cm

   A 11 square centimeters
   B 22 square centimeters
   C 24 square centimeters
   D 28 square centimeters

Reporting Category 3
Geometry and Measurement

Exercise 13

3.6C: Determine the area of rectangles with whole number side lengths in problems using multiplication related to the number of rows times the number of unit squares in each row (Readiness Standard)

(3.1F)
1. What is the area of the diagram below?

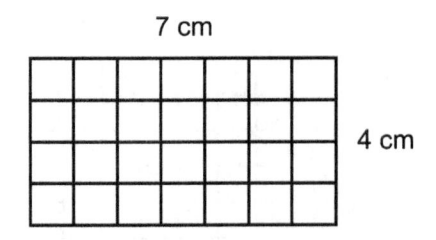

   7 cm
   4 cm

   A 11 square centimeters
   B 22 square centimeters
   C 24 square centimeters
   D 28 square centimeters

(3.1F)
2. What is the area of the diagram below?

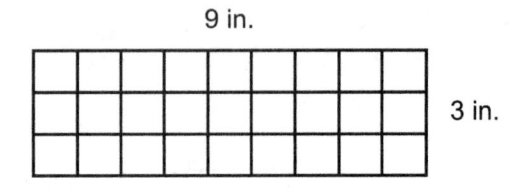

   9 in.
   3 in.

   A 24 square inches
   B 27 square inches
   C 29 square inches
   D 36 square inches

(3.1F)
3. Which diagram has an area of 32 square inches?

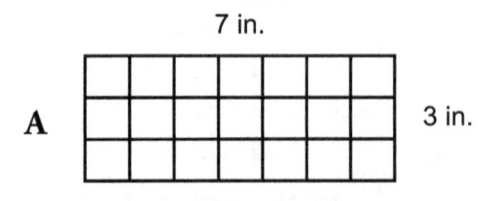

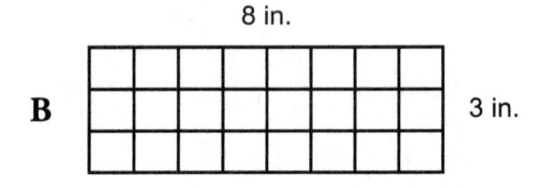

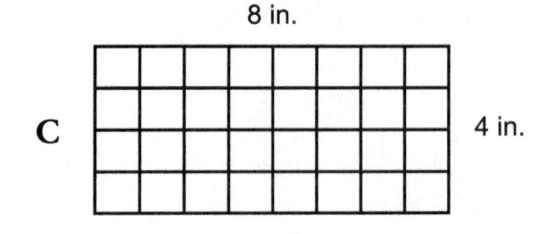

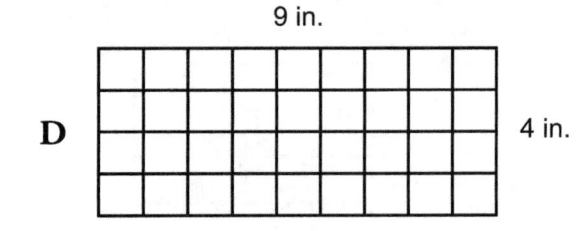

   A   7 in. 3 in.

   B   8 in. 3 in.

   C   8 in. 4 in.

   D   9 in. 4 in.

110   STAAR MASTER® Student Practice Book—Math, Grade 3   © ECS Learning Systems, Inc.

Reporting Category 3
Geometry and Measurement

Exercise 14

3.6D: Decompose composite figures formed by rectangles into non-overlapping rectangles to determine the area of the original figure using the additive property of area (Supporting Standard)

(3.1F)
1. What is the area of the figure below?

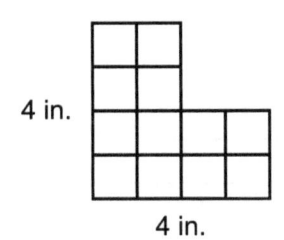

   4 in.
   4 in.

   A 8 square inches
   B 12 square inches
   C 16 square inches
   D 20 square inches

(3.1F)
2. What is the area of the figure below?

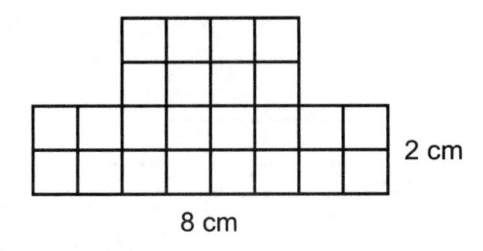

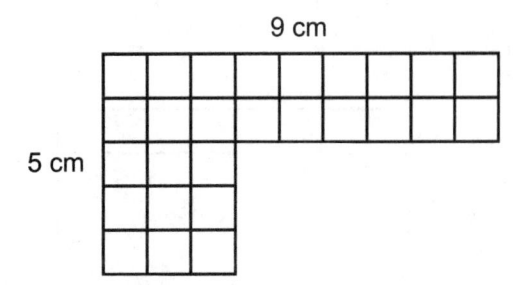

   2 cm
   8 cm

   A 16 square centimeters
   B 20 square centimeters
   C 24 square centimeters
   D 32 square centimeters

(3.1F)
3. What is the area of the figure below?

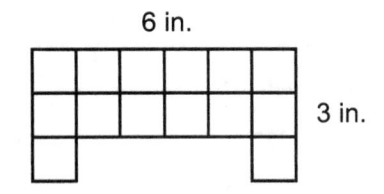

   6 in.
   3 in.

   A 12 square inches
   B 14 square inches
   C 18 square inches
   D 20 square inches

(3.1F)
4. What is the area of the figure below?

   9 cm
   5 cm

   A 14 square centimeters
   B 18 square centimeters
   C 27 square centimeters
   D 45 square centimeters

Reporting Category 3
Geometry and Measurement

Exercise 15

3.6D: Decompose composite figures formed by rectangles into non-overlapping rectangles to determine the area of the original figure using the additive property of area (Supporting Standard)

(3.1F)
1. What is the area of the figure below?

   10 cm
   4 cm

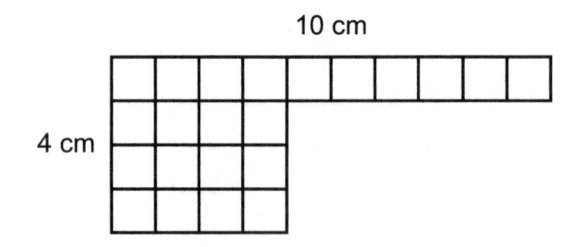

   A   14 square centimeters
   B   22 square centimeters
   C   28 square centimeters
   D   40 square centimeters

(3.1F)
2. What is the area of the figure below?

   8 in.
   5 in.

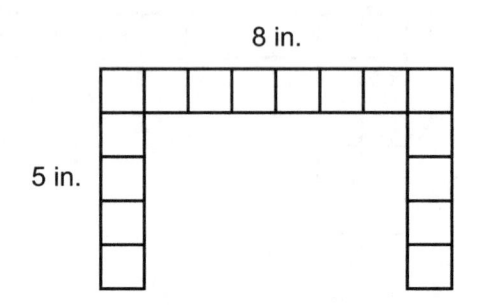

   A   26 square inches
   B   18 square inches
   C   16 square inches
   D   13 square inches

(3.1F)
3. What is the area of the figure below?

   5 cm
   7 cm

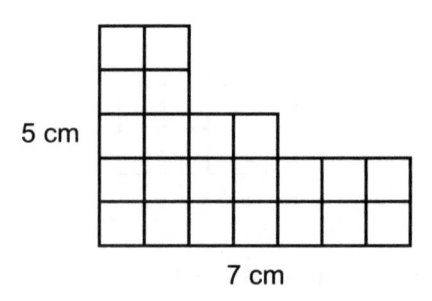

   A   12 square centimeters
   B   16 square centimeters
   C   20 square centimeters
   D   22 square centimeters

(3.1F)
4. What is the area of the figure below?

   3 in.
   8 in.

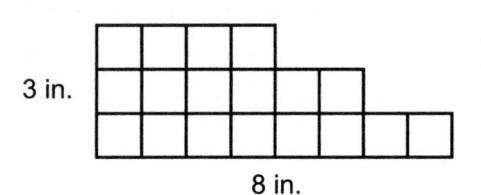

   A   11 square inches
   B   16 square inches
   C   18 square inches
   D   24 square inches

Reporting Category 3
Geometry and Measurement

Exercise 16

3.6E: Decompose two congruent two-dimensional figures into parts with equal areas and express the area of each part as a unit fraction of the whole, and recognize that equal shares of identical wholes need not have the same shape (Supporting Standard)

(3.1F)

1. Look at rectangle A below. Half of the rectangle is shaded.

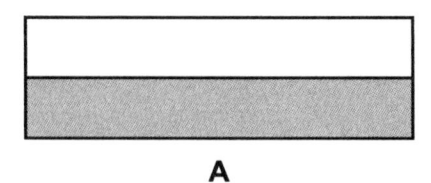

   A

   Each rectangle below has the same size and shape as rectangle A. In which rectangle is the same area shaded?

   A

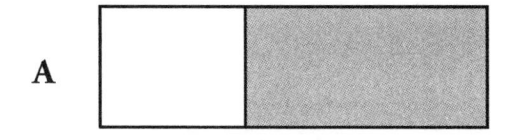

   B

   C

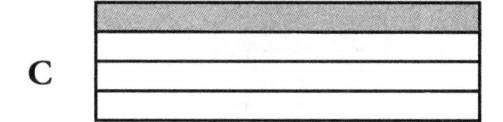

   D

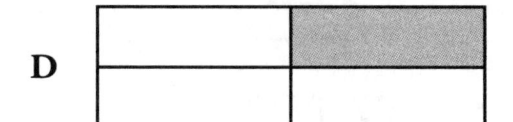

(3.1F)

2. In which figures are the shaded areas equal?

   A

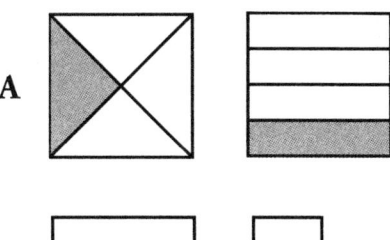

   B

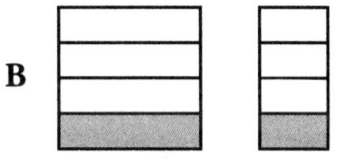

   C

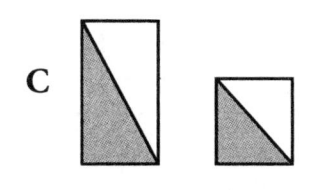

   D

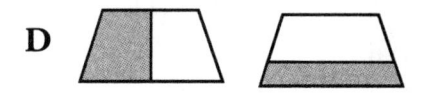

Reporting Category 3
Geometry and Measurement

Exercise 17

3.6E: Decompose two congruent two-dimensional figures into parts with equal areas and express the area of each part as a unit fraction of the whole, and recognize that equal shares of identical wholes need not have the same shape (Supporting Standard)

(3.1F)

1. In which figures are the shaded areas equal?

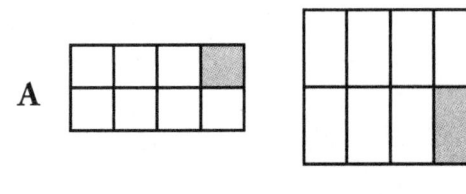

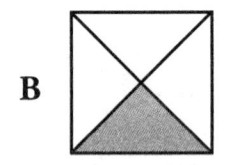

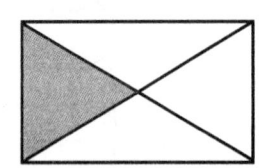

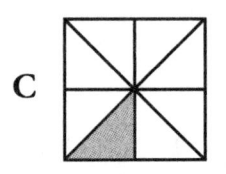

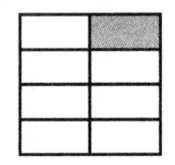

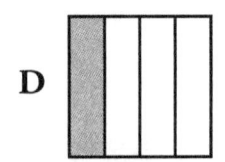

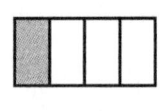

   A

   B

   C

   D

(3.1F)

2. Look at square A below. The square is divided into sixths, and $\frac{1}{6}$ is shaded.

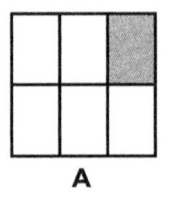

   A

   Each square below is the same size as square A. In which square does the shaded area equal square A's shaded area?

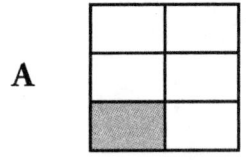

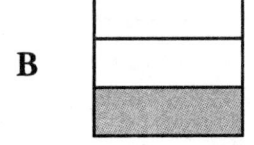

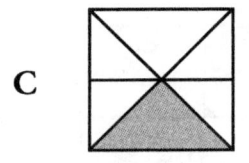

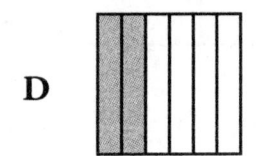

   A

   B

   C

   D

---

114   STAAR MASTER® Student Practice Book—Math, Grade 3   © ECS Learning Systems, Inc.

Reporting Category 3
Geometry and Measurement

Exercise 18

3.7B: Determine the perimeter of a polygon or a missing length when given perimeter and remaining side lengths in problems (Readiness Standard)

(3.1A; 3.1B; 3.1F)

1. Felix and Javier wanted to know who ran the greatest distance around the block. Look at their paths below.

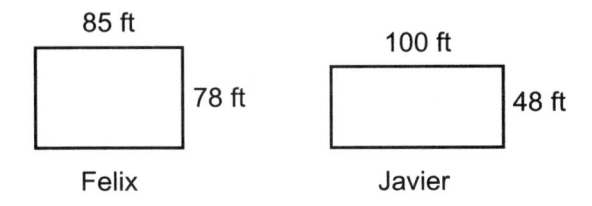

   Felix: 85 ft, 78 ft
   Javier: 100 ft, 48 ft

   Which expression shows one way to determine who ran the greatest distance?

   A 100 + 100 + 48 + 48
   B 85 + 85 + 78 + 78
   C 163 − 148
   D 326 − 296

(3.1B; 3.1F)

2. The perimeter of the rectangle below is 22 centimeters. The length of the rectangle is 6 centimeters.

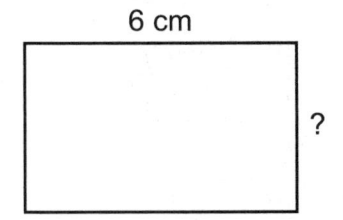

   6 cm, ?

   What is the width of the rectangle?

   A 5 cm
   B 10 cm
   C 12 cm
   D 16 cm

(3.1B; 3.1F)

3. The polygon below has a perimeter of 23 centimeters.

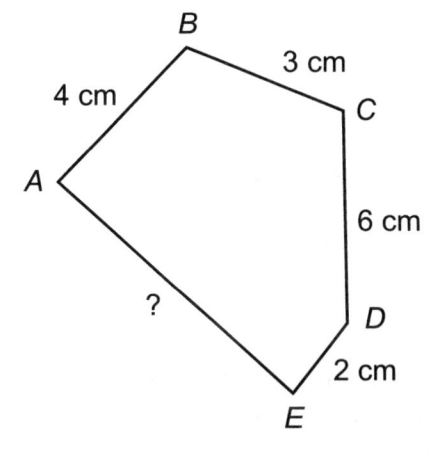

   AB = 4 cm, BC = 3 cm, CD = 6 cm, DE = 2 cm, EA = ?

   What is the distance from A to E?

   A 8 cm
   B 10 cm
   C 12 cm
   D 15 cm

(3.1F)

4. Each side of a square measures 4 inches. What is the perimeter of the square?

   A 20 inches
   B 16 inches
   C 12 inches
   D 8 inches

Reporting Category 3
Geometry and Measurement

Exercise 19

3.7B: Determine the perimeter of a polygon or a missing length when given perimeter and remaining side lengths in problems (Readiness Standard)

(3.1F)
1. A rectangle has a length of 7 centimeters and a width of 5 centimeters. What is the perimeter of the rectangle?

   A 12 cm
   B 17 cm
   C 24 cm
   D 35 cm

(3.1A; 3.1F)
2. Candice was comparing the perimeter of two items she found in her room at home.

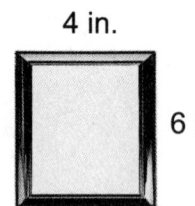

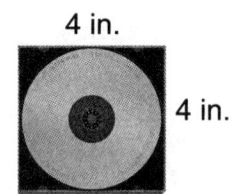

   4 in.   4 in.

   6 in.   4 in.

   What is the combined perimeter of Candice's items?

   A 14 in.
   B 18 in.
   C 36 in.
   D 40 in.

(3.1F)
3. What is the perimeter of the shape below?

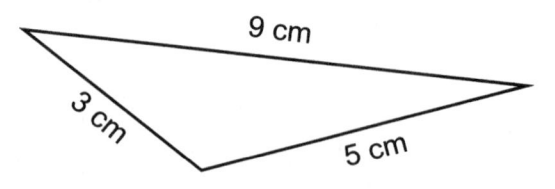

   9 cm
   3 cm
   5 cm

   A 8 cm
   B 12 cm
   C 14 cm
   D 17 cm

(3.1F)
4. Look at the figure below.

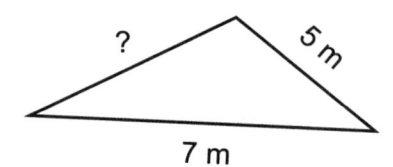

   ?   5 m
   7 m

   The perimeter of the shape is 18 meters. What is the length of the missing side?

   A 5 m
   B 6 m
   C 7 m
   D 8 m

Reporting Category 3
Geometry and Measurement

Exercise 20

3.7B: Determine the perimeter of a polygon or a missing length when given perimeter and remaining side lengths in problems (Readiness Standard)

(3.1F)
1. What is the perimeter of the figure below?

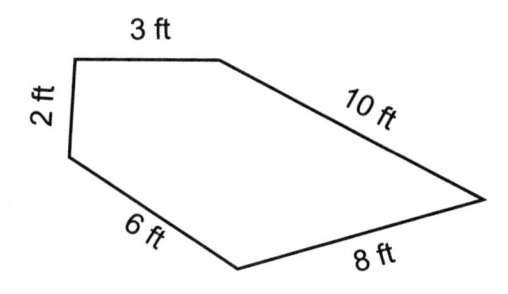

   3 ft
   2 ft
   10 ft
   6 ft
   8 ft

   A 19 ft
   B 23 ft
   C 26 ft
   D 29 ft

(3.1F)
2. Look at the rectangle below.

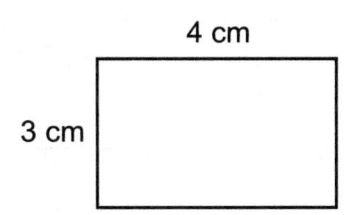

   4 cm
   3 cm

   What is the perimeter of the rectangle?

   A 9 cm
   B 10 cm
   C 12 cm
   D 14 cm

(3.1A; 3.1F)
3. The perimeter of a tabletop is 14 feet. If the table is 5 feet long, what is the table's width?

   A 1 foot
   B 2 feet
   C 4 feet
   D 9 feet

(3.1A; 3.1F)
4. Jeff is installing a fence around his entire yard. A diagram of Jeff's yard is shown below.

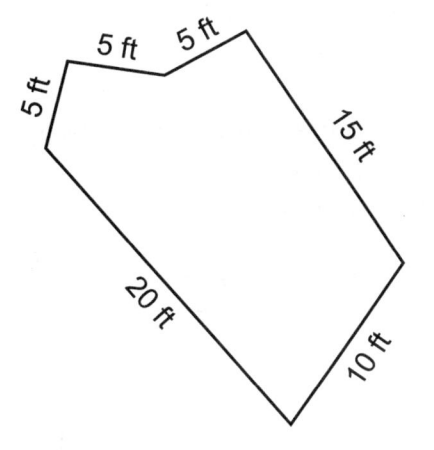

   5 ft
   5 ft
   5 ft
   15 ft
   20 ft
   10 ft

   How many feet of fencing does Jeff need for his yard?

   Record your answer in the boxes. Then fill in the bubbles. Be sure to use the correct place value.

Reporting Category 3
Geometry and Measurement

Exercise 21

3.7B: Determine the perimeter of a polygon or a missing length when given perimeter and remaining side lengths in problems (Readiness Standard)

(3.1F)
1. What is the perimeter of the regular hexagon below?

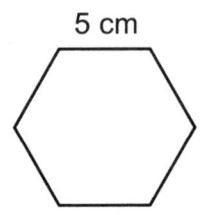

   5 cm

   A 5 cm
   B 10 cm
   C 30 cm
   D 40 cm

(3.1A; 3.1F)
2. The Lopez family is planning to put a rectangular pool in their backyard. The perimeter of the pool is 60 feet.

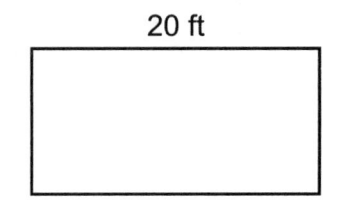

   20 ft

   The width of the pool is—

   A 10 ft
   B 20 ft
   C 60 ft
   D 120 ft

(3.1A; 3.1F)
3. The perimeter of the square baseball field at Josh's school is 360 feet.

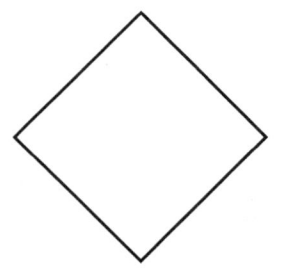

   How long is each side of the field?

   A 40 ft
   B 90 ft
   C 180 ft
   D 360 ft

(3.1A; 3.1F)
4. Mrs. Wilson is making a birthday cake for her daughter Lisa. The recipe suggests using a 13 × 9-inch pan. What is the perimeter of the pan, in inches?

   Record your answer in the boxes. Then fill in the bubbles. Be sure to use the correct place value.

Reporting Category 3
Geometry and Measurement

Exercise 22

3.7C: Determine the solutions to problems involving addition and subtraction of time intervals in minutes using pictorial models or tools such as a 15-minute event plus a 30-minute event equals 45 minutes (Supporting Standard)

(3.1A; 3.1C)

1. Tammy is waiting for the school bus, which normally comes at the time shown below.

   She looks at her watch and sees she has 10 more minutes to wait for the bus. What time is it when Tammy looks at her watch?

   A 6:05   C 6:15
   B 6:10   D 6:20

(3.1A; 3.1C)

2. Scott is waiting for a train scheduled to arrive at 12:30. When he looks at his watch to see how much time he has left to wait, he sees the time shown below.

   How much longer will Scott wait for the train?

   A 10 min   C 20 min
   B 15 min   D 30 min

(3.1A; 3.1D; 3.1F)

3. Each night, Debbie practices piano for 20 minutes and reads for 15 minutes. Which number line shows the total amount of time Debbie spends reading and practicing piano each night?

   A 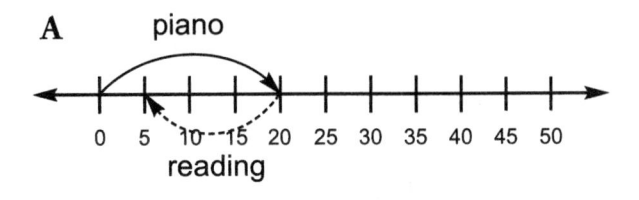
   B 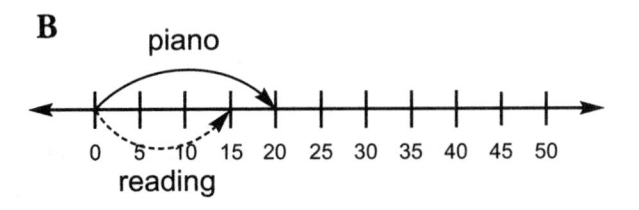
   C 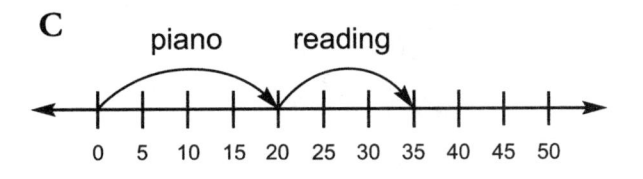
   D

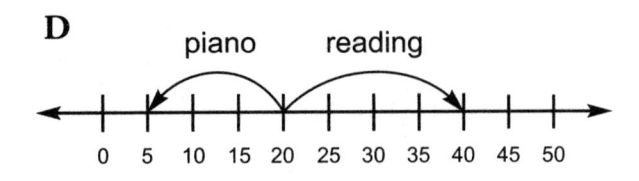

Reporting Category 3
Geometry and Measurement

Exercise 23

3.7C: Determine the solutions to problems involving addition and subtraction of time intervals in minutes using pictorial models or tools such as a 15-minute event plus a 30-minute event equals 45 minutes (Supporting Standard)

(3.1A; 3.1B; 3.1E; 3.1F)

1. Mrs. Luna finished several chores on Monday. The table below shows the chores she did and how much time she spent on three of them.

Mrs. Luna's Chores

Chore	Time Spent (in minutes)
Vacuuming	20
Dusting	10
Laundry	45
Making Beds	
Total Time	**85 minutes**

How much time did Mrs. Luna spend making beds on Monday?

A 5 minutes
B 10 minutes
C 15 minutes
D 20 minutes

(3.1A; 3.1B; 3.1D; 3.1F)

2. The diagram below shows how much time Jeff usually spends getting to school.

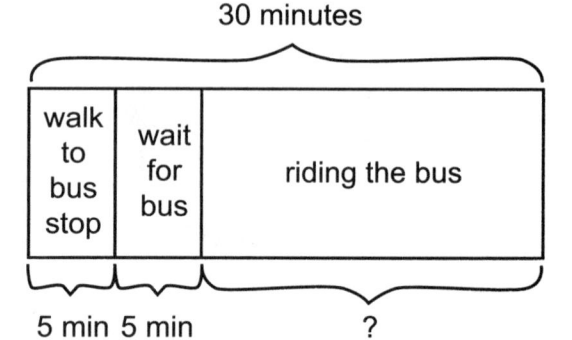

Based on the diagram, how much time does Jeff usually spend riding the bus to school?

A 10 minutes
B 15 minutes
C 20 minutes
D 30 minutes

(3.1A; 3.1C; 3.1F)

3. Mr. Mason drives 45 minutes every day from his home to work. He leaves his house at the time shown below.

At what time does Mr. Mason arrive at work?

A 7:45
B 8:00
C 8:15
D 8:25

Reporting Category 3
Geometry and Measurement

Exercise 24

3.7C: Determine the solutions to problems involving addition and subtraction of time intervals in minutes using pictorial models or tools such as a 15-minute event plus a 30-minute event equals 45 minutes (Supporting Standard)

(3.1A; 3.1B; 3.1D; 3.1F)

1. The diagram below shows how much time Mrs. Jensen spent at her hair appointment.

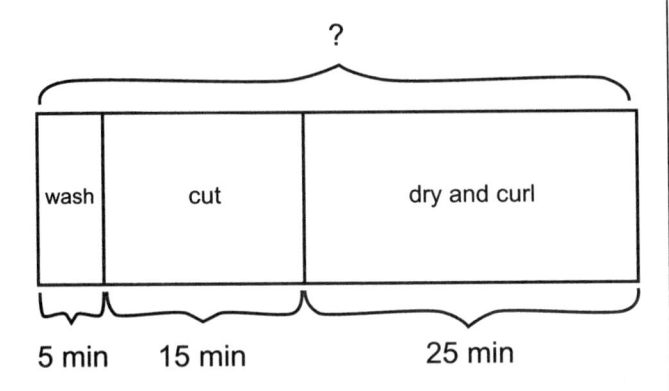

   | ? |
   | wash | cut | dry and curl |
   | 5 min | 15 min | 25 min |

   Based on the diagram, how long was Mrs. Jensen at her hair appointment?

   A 20 minutes
   B 25 minutes
   C 35 minutes
   D 45 minutes

The number line below shows the amount of time Ellen spent on her homework in different subjects. Use the number line to answer questions 2 and 3.

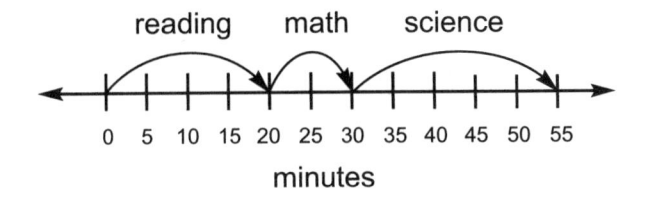

reading   math   science
0 5 10 15 20 25 30 35 40 45 50 55
minutes

(3.1A; 3.1D; 3.1F)

2. How much more time did Ellen spend on reading and math homework combined than on science homework?

   A 5 minutes
   B 10 minutes
   C 15 minutes
   D 20 minutes

(3.1A; 3.1D; 3.1F)

3. How much time did Ellen spend on math homework?

   A 5 minutes
   B 10 minutes
   C 25 minutes
   D 30 minutes

Reporting Category 3
Geometry and Measurement

Exercise 25

3.7D: Determine when it is appropriate to use measurements of liquid volume (capacity) or weight (Supporting Standard)

Adele and her mother shopped at a grocery store. Answer questions 1–4 about their shopping.

(3.1A; 3.1F)
1. Which item did Adele and her mother most likely buy according to its weight?

   A Milk
   B Orange juice
   C Potatoes
   D Yogurt

(3.1A; 3.1F)
2. Adele's mother wanted to buy butter. Butter is most often sold by the—

   A gallon
   B liter
   C pound
   D quart

(3.1A; 3.1F)
3. Adele and her mother most likely bought each of the following items by the pound **EXCEPT**—

   A bananas
   B meat
   C onions
   D water

(3.1A; 3.1F)
4. Adele and her mother bought the box of cookies shown below.

   Cookies
   Contents: 7 pouches
   210 _____ ← unit of measure

   What unit of measure most likely follows the number 210 on the front of the box?

   A Grams
   B Milliliters
   C Pints
   D Quarts

Reporting Category 3
Geometry and Measurement

Exercise 26

3.7D: Determine when it is appropriate to use measurements of liquid volume (capacity) or weight (Supporting Standard)

(3.1C)
1. Which of the following tools would most likely be used to measure the amount of water in a pitcher?

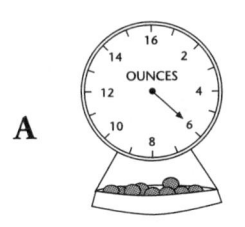

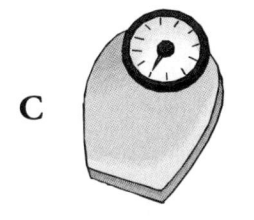

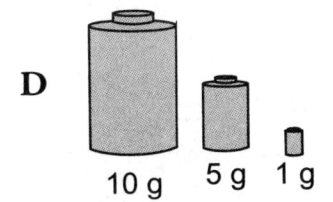

   A

   B

   C

   D

(3.1A; 3.1F)
2. Jarod took a package to the post office. The clerk weighed the package and told Jarod how much postage he needed to pay.

   The clerk most likely weighed the package in—

   A pints and quarts
   B ounces and cups
   C milliliters and liters
   D ounces and pounds

(3.1A; 3.1F)
3. When John bought soft drinks at the store, he most likely bought them by the—

   A gram
   B kilogram
   C liter
   D pound

Reporting Category 3
Geometry and Measurement

Exercise 27

3.7E: Determine liquid volume (capacity) or weight using appropriate units and tools (Supporting Standard)

(3.1A; 3.1C)

1. Mrs. Muñoz bought the clay shown below for her art students.

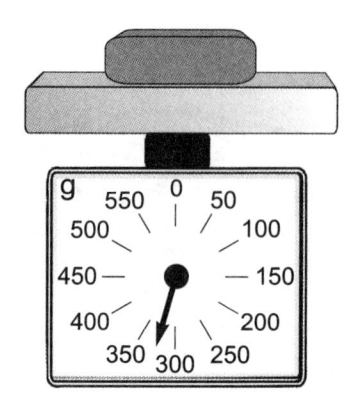

   How much clay did Mrs. Muñoz buy?

   A 275 g C 325 g
   B 300 g D 350 g

(3.1A; 3.1C)

2. Clare and Marna each did a science experiment. The amounts of water they used for their experiments are shown below.

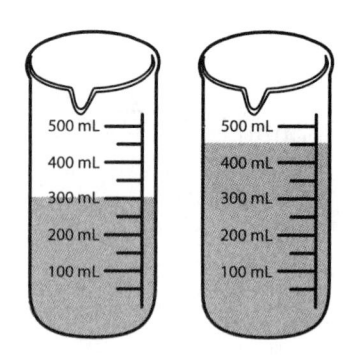

   How much water did the girls use in all?

   A 300 mL C 750 mL
   B 450 mL D 850 mL

(3.1A; 3.1C)

3. A truck driver stopped to have his vehicle weighed, as shown below.

   How much did the vehicle weigh?

   A $4\frac{1}{2}$ tons

   B 5 tons

   C $5\frac{1}{2}$ tons

   D 6 tons

(3.1A; 3.1C)

4. Every day, Mrs. Tanner's children each drink the amount of milk shown below.

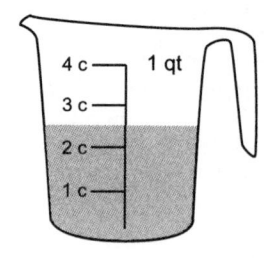

   How much milk does each child drink per day?

   A 1 cup   C 2 cups
   B $1\frac{1}{2}$ cups   D $2\frac{1}{2}$ cups

Reporting Category 3
Geometry and Measurement

Exercise 28

3.7E: Determine liquid volume (capacity) or weight using appropriate units and tools (Supporting Standard)

(3.1A; 3.1C)

1. Gabe poured 50 milliliters of water into his fishbowl. Which of the following shows the amount of water Gabe used to fill his fishbowl?

    A

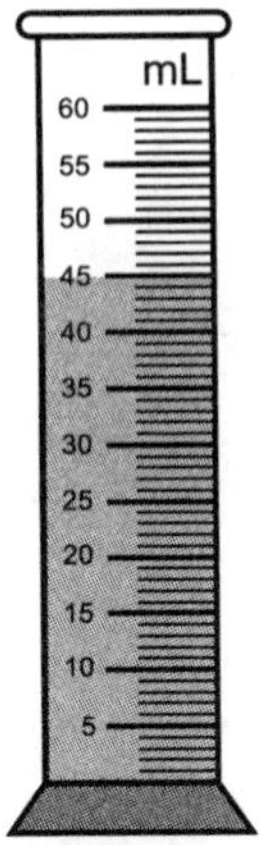

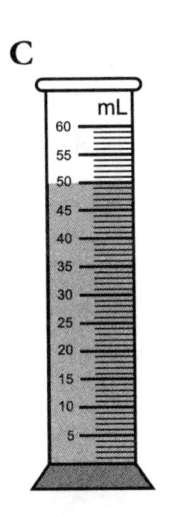

    B

    C

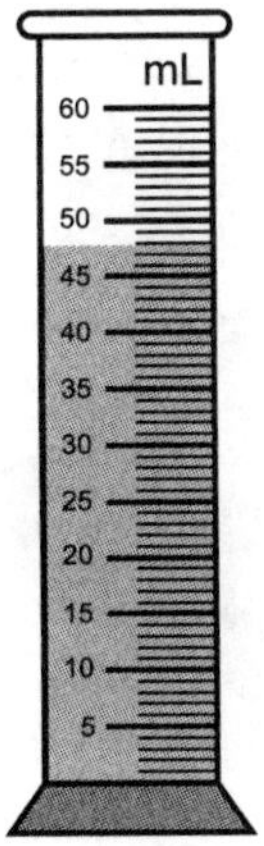

    D

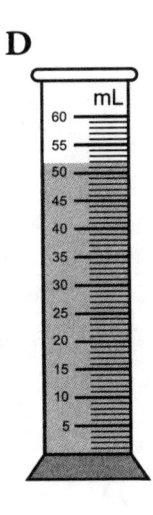

(3.1A; 3.1C)

2. Martin bought the apples shown on the scale below.

    How much did the apples Martin bought weigh?

    A 14 oz   C 16 oz
    B 15 oz   D 17 oz

(3.1A; 3.1C)

3. In science class, Jennifer measured the liquid shown below.

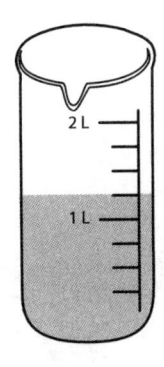

    How much liquid did Jennifer measure?

    A $1\frac{1}{4}$ liters   C $2\frac{1}{4}$ liters
    B $1\frac{3}{4}$ liters   D $2\frac{3}{4}$ liters

Reporting Category 3
Geometry and Measurement

Exercise 29

3.7E: Determine liquid volume (capacity) or weight using appropriate units and tools (Supporting Standard)

(3.1A; 3.1C)

1. Jamie's mom made fruit punch for Jamie and his friends. The amount of punch she made is shown below.

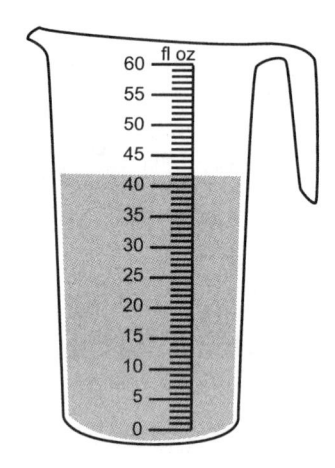

   How much fruit punch did Jamie's mom make?

   A 38 fl oz **C** 48 fl oz
   B 42 fl oz **D** 52 fl oz

(3.1A; 3.1C)

2. Nick weighed a book that he wanted to mail. The book's weight is shown below.

   How much does Nick's book weigh?

   A 25 oz **C** 33 oz
   B 27 oz **D** 37 oz

(3.1A; 3.1C)

3. Melanie and Tito picked 190 grams of strawberries together. Which scale below shows the strawberries Melanie and Tito picked?

   A 175 g

   B 190 g

   C 205 g

   D 210 g

Reporting Category 4
Data Analysis and Personal Financial Literacy

3.4   C. Determine the value of a collection of coins and bills (Supporting Standard)

3.8   A. Summarize a data set with multiple categories using a frequency table, dot plot, pictograph, or bar graph with scaled intervals (Readiness Standard)

      B. Solve one- and two-step problems using categorical data represented with a frequency table, dot plot, pictograph, or bar graph with scaled intervals (Supporting Standard)

3.9   A. Explain the connection between human capital/labor and income (Supporting Standard)

      B. Describe the relationship between the availability or scarcity of resources and how that impacts cost (Supporting Standard)

      D. Explain that credit is used when wants or needs exceed the ability to pay and that it is the borrower's responsibility to pay it back to the lender, usually with interest (Supporting Standard)

      E. List reasons to save, and explain the benefit of a savings plan, including for college (Supporting Standard)

Reporting Category 4
Data Analysis and Personal Financial Literacy

Exercise 1

3.4C: Determine the value of a collection of coins and bills (Supporting Standard)

(3.1A; 3.1F)

1. Tara needs 40¢ to buy a snack. Which set of coins equals 40¢?

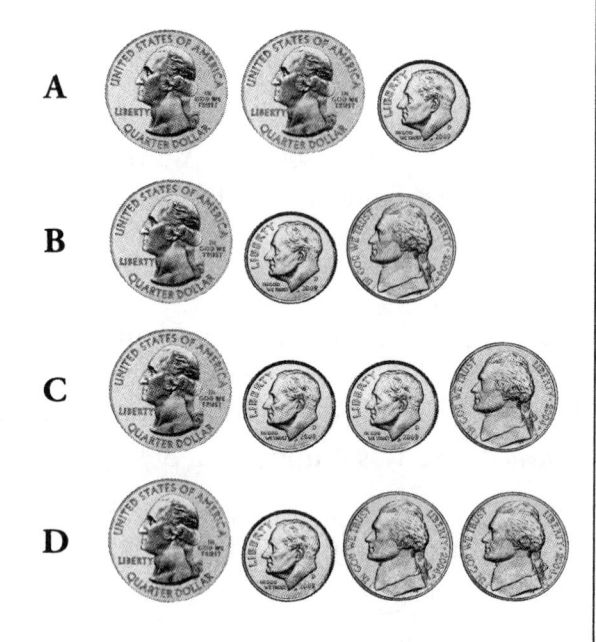

   A (quarter, quarter, dime)

   B (quarter, dime, nickel)

   C (quarter, dime, nickel, nickel)

   D (quarter, dime, nickel, nickel)

(3.1A; 3.1F)

2. Landon gave a clerk $1.00 and received 26¢ in change. Which set of coins equals 26¢?

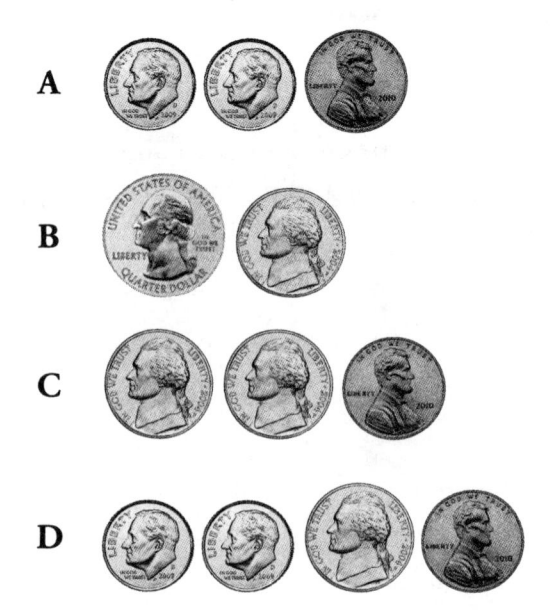

   A (dime, dime, penny)

   B (quarter, penny)

   C (nickel, nickel, penny)

   D (dime, dime, nickel, penny)

(3.1F)

3. What is the total value of the coins shown below?

   (quarter, quarter, quarter, dime, nickel, penny)

   A 86¢   C 95¢
   B 91¢   D $1.00

The chart below shows how many coins different children have. Use the chart to answer questions 4 and 5.

Child	quarter	dime	nickel	penny
Cindy	1	3	2	0
Jade	2	0	1	3
Luke	0	3	1	4
Zach	3	1	0	2

(3.1A; 3.1D; 3.1F)

4. Which child has exactly 39¢?

   A Cindy   C Luke
   B Jade   D Zach

(3.1A; 3.1D; 3.1F)

5. Which child has the most money?

   A Cindy   C Luke
   B Jade   D Zach

128 STAAR MASTER® Student Practice Book—Math, Grade 3 © ECS Learning Systems, Inc.

Reporting Category 4
Data Analysis and Personal Financial Literacy

Exercise 2

3.4C: Determine the value of a collection of coins and bills (Supporting Standard)

(3.1A; 3.1F)

1. Mr. Morgan found the coins below in his pocket.

   What is the value of the coins Mr. Morgan found in his pocket?

   A 28¢
   B 80¢
   C 88¢
   D 98¢

(3.1A; 3.1F)

2. Allison bought shoelaces with the money shown below.

   How much did Allison pay for the shoelaces?

   A $2.56   C $2.84
   B $2.79   D $2.95

(3.1A; 3.1F)

3. Jan found the coins below in her desk.

   Which group of coins shows the same amount of money that Jan found?

   A

   B

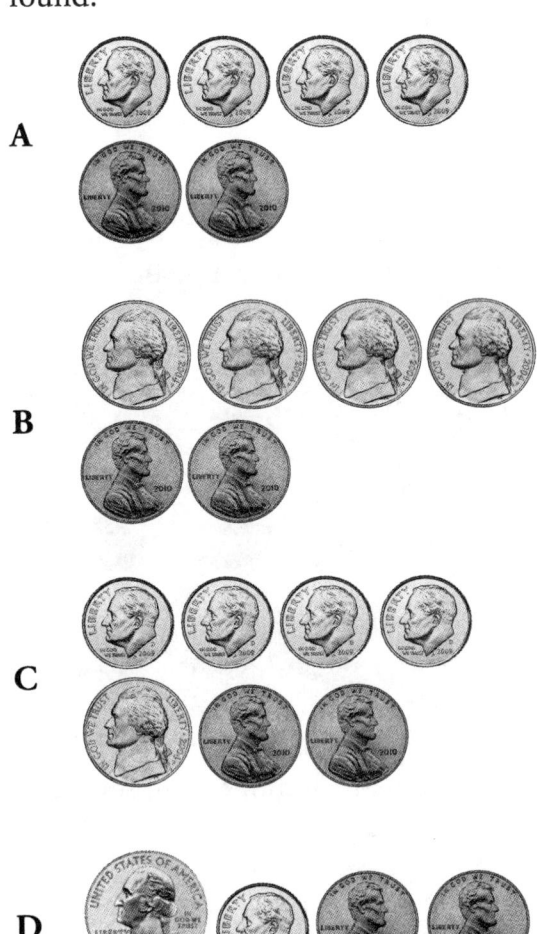

   C

   D

Reporting Category 4
Data Analysis and Personal Financial Literacy

Exercise 3

3.4C: Determine the value of a collection of coins and bills (Supporting Standard)

(3.1F)
1. What is the value of the coins shown below?

   A 66¢
   B 71¢
   C 81¢
   D $1.11

(3.1A; 3.1F)
2. Tanya has the coins shown below.

   If Tanya loses 1 nickel and 1 penny, how much money will she have left?

   A 71¢
   B 75¢
   C 85¢
   D 91¢

(3.1F)
3. How much money is shown below?

   A 33¢
   B 36¢
   C 42¢
   D 46¢

(3.1A; 3.1F)
4. Megan paid for a carton of milk with the money shown below.

   How much did Megan pay for the milk?

   A $1.17
   B $1.18
   C $1.35
   D $1.40

Reporting Category 4
Data Analysis and Personal Financial Literacy

Exercise 4

3.8A: Summarize a data set with multiple categories using a frequency table, dot plot, pictograph, or bar graph with scaled intervals (Readiness Standard)

(3.1A; 3.1D; 3.1F)

1. The frequency table below shows the numbers of baseball cards each of 3 students have.

Baseball Cards Owned

Student	Colby	Sue	Tom
Number of Cards	llll llll	llll	llll llll llll

Which graph matches the facts given in the chart?

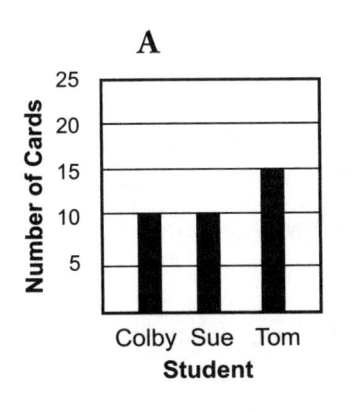

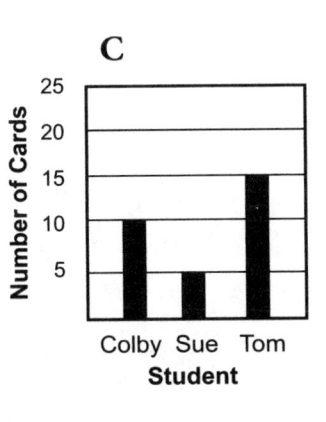

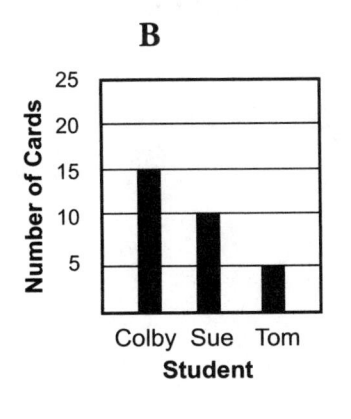

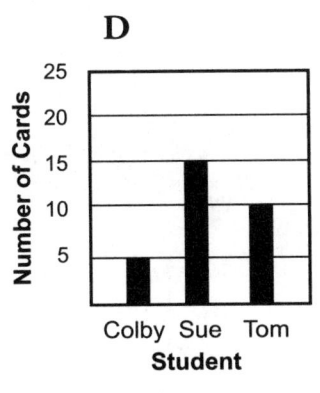

A
(bar graph: Colby 10, Sue 10, Tom 15)

B
(bar graph: Colby 15, Sue 10, Tom 5)

C
(bar graph: Colby 10, Sue 5, Tom 15)

D
(bar graph: Colby 5, Sue 15, Tom 10)

Use the information below to answer questions 2 and 3.

The dot plot shows how much money students raised for a school fundraiser.

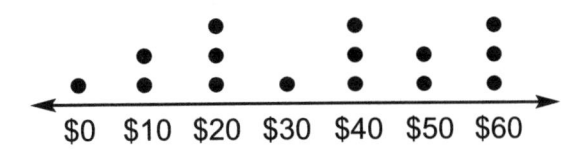

(dot plot: $0: 1 dot, $10: 3 dots, $20: 3 dots, $30: 2 dots, $40: 3 dots, $50: 3 dots, $60: 3 dots)

Money Raised by Students

(3.1A; 3.1D; 3.1F)

2. How many students raised $40 or more for the school fundraiser?

   A 3
   B 5
   C 8
   D 10

(3.1A; 3.1D; 3.1F)

3. The dot plot shows how much money was raised by—

   A 7 students
   B 8 students
   C 14 students
   D 15 students

Reporting Category 4
Data Analysis and Personal Financial Literacy

Exercise 5

3.8A: Summarize a data set with multiple categories using a frequency table, dot plot, pictograph, or bar graph with scaled intervals (Readiness Standard)

(3.1A; 3.1D)

1. The Rodriguez family went shopping for clothes. The chart below shows what each person bought.

Jessica	4 shirts	2 pants
Sandra	2 sweaters	
Mrs. Rodriguez	1 skirt	2 pants
Mr. Rodriguez	3 sweaters	2 shirts

Which tally chart correctly shows the information from the chart above?

A

Clothes	Tally
Shirts	⊮ I
Pants	IIII
Sweaters	⊮
Skirts	I

B

Clothes	Tally
Shirts	IIII
Pants	IIII
Sweaters	⊮
Skirts	I

C

Clothes	Tally
Shirts	⊮
Pants	IIII
Sweaters	III
Skirts	I

D

Clothes	Tally
Shirts	⊮ I
Pants	II
Sweaters	⊮
Skirts	I

(3.1A; 3.1D; 3.1F; 3.1G)

2. Visha wants to find the number of days it rained in Brownsville last month.

Rain in Brownsville

Sunny	✿ ✿ ✿ ✿
Rainy	✿
Cloudy	✿
Windy	✿ ✿

✿ = 5 days

What should she do to find the number of days it rained?

A Add 5 days to the number of ✿.

B Subtract 5 days from the number of ✿.

C Multiply the number of ✿ by 5.

D Divide the number of ✿ by 5.

Reporting Category 4
Data Analysis and Personal Financial Literacy

Exercise 6

3.8A: Summarize a data set with multiple categories using a frequency table, dot plot, pictograph, or bar graph with scaled intervals (Readiness Standard)

(3.1A; 3.1D; 3.1F)

1. Dorothy was passing out flyers in her neighborhood. The number of houses she visited is shown below.

Flyers Passed Out

Day	Houses Visited
Monday	🏠 🏠
Tuesday	🏠 🏠 🏠
Wednesday	🏠
Thursday	🏠 🏠 🏠 🏠
Friday	🏠 🏠 🏠 🏠 🏠

🏠 = 5 houses

How many more houses did Dorothy visit on Thursday than on Tuesday?

A 1
B 5
C 25
D 35

(3.1A; 3.1D; 3.1F)

2. Connie kept track of the number of people who came to the school play each day. The results are shown in the table below.

School Play Attendance

Day	Number of People
Monday	150
Tuesday	225
Wednesday	200
Thursday	175
Friday	250

Connie wants to put this information on a graph. Which of the following blank graphs would be the best one for Connie to use?

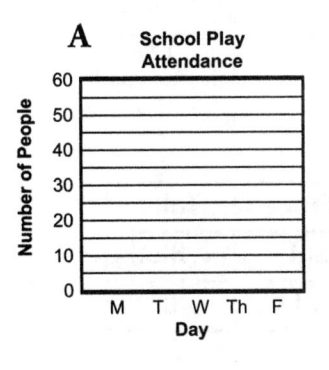

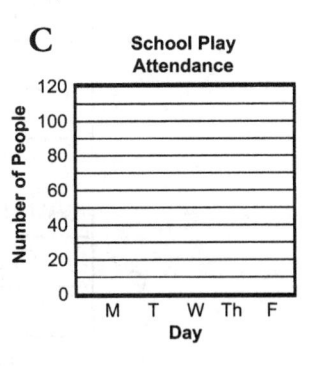

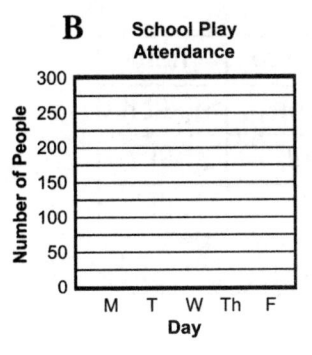

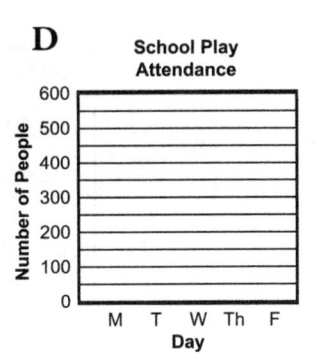

A School Play Attendance (0–60, by 10s)

B School Play Attendance (0–300, by 50s)

C School Play Attendance (0–120, by 20s)

D School Play Attendance (0–600, by 100s)

Reporting Category 4
Data Analysis and Personal Financial Literacy

Exercise 7

3.8A: Summarize a data set with multiple categories using a frequency table, dot plot, pictograph, or bar graph with scaled intervals (Readiness Standard)

(3.1A; 3.1D; 3.1F)

1. Four children listed their school attendance records for last week.

Kenneth	5 present
Isabel	4 present and 1 absent
Rita	3 present and 1 late
Ally	3 present, 1 absent, and 1 late

Which tally chart correctly shows the information the children listed?

A

Attendance	Tally
Present	𝍤 𝍤 II
Absent	II
Late	III

B

Attendance	Tally
Present	𝍤 𝍤 𝍤
Absent	I
Late	III

C

Attendance	Tally
Present	𝍤 𝍤 𝍤
Absent	II
Late	II

D

Attendance	Tally
Present	𝍤 𝍤 𝍤
Absent	III
Late	III

(3.1A; 3.1D; 3.1F)

2. For a survey, a teacher asked her students to choose their favorite pets. The dot plot below shows the results of the survey.

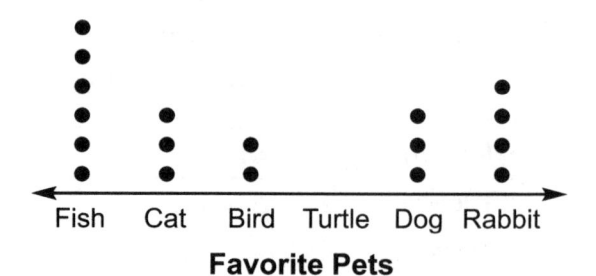

Favorite Pets
Fish, Cat, Bird, Turtle, Dog, Rabbit

How many students were surveyed?

A 6   C 15
B 10   D 18

(3.1A; 3.1D; 3.1F; 3.1G)

3. The school cafeteria keeps track of how many cartons of milk students drink at lunchtime. The results are shown on the graph below.

Lunch Milk

Day	Number of Cartons
Monday	🥛🥛🥛🥛🥛
Tuesday	🥛🥛🥛🥛🥛🥛
Wednesday	🥛🥛🥛🥛🥛
Thursday	🥛🥛🥛🥛
Friday	🥛🥛🥛🥛🥛🥛

If students drank 120 cartons of milk on Monday, how many cartons of milk does one 🥛 represent?

A 10   C 30
B 20   D 40

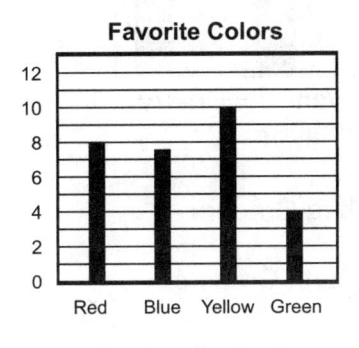

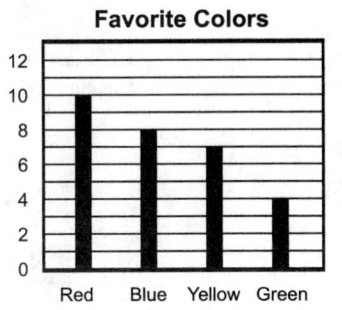

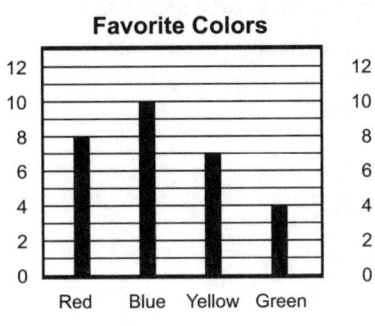

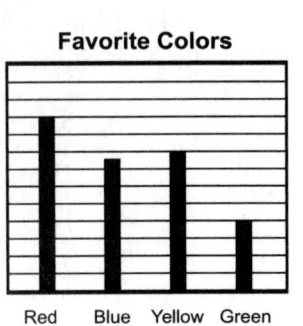

Reporting Category 4
Data Analysis and Personal Financial Literacy

Exercise 8

3.8A: Summarize a data set with multiple categories using a frequency table, dot plot, pictograph, or bar graph with scaled intervals (Readiness Standard)

Use the information below to answer questions 1 and 2.

The graph below shows several students' favorite pizza toppings.

Favorite Pizza Toppings

Topping	Number of Votes
Pepperoni	🍕 🍕 🍕 (half)
Sausage	🍕 (half)
Cheese	🍕 🍕 🍕
Mushrooms	🍕

🍕 = 4 votes

(3.1A; 3.1D; 3.1F)

1. How many students voted for a favorite pizza topping?

   A 8
   B 18
   C 32
   D 36

(3.1A; 3.1D; 3.1F)

2. How many students chose cheese as their favorite pizza topping?

   A 3
   B 6
   C 12
   D 15

(3.1A; 3.1D; 3.1F)

3. Brenda asked her classmates to name their favorite colors. The results are shown below.

Favorite Colors

Color	Number of Votes
Red	||||| |||||
Blue	||||| |||
Yellow	||||| ||
Green	||||

Which graph correctly shows the information Brenda gathered?

A, B, C, D (bar graphs of Favorite Colors)

Reporting Category 4
Data Analysis and Personal Financial Literacy

Exercise 9

3.8B: Solve one- and two-step problems using categorical data represented with a frequency table, dot plot, pictograph, or bar graph with scaled intervals (Supporting Standard)

Use the graph below to answer questions 1–4.

The graph shows the number of ice cream cones sold to third- and fourth-grade students during lunch time.

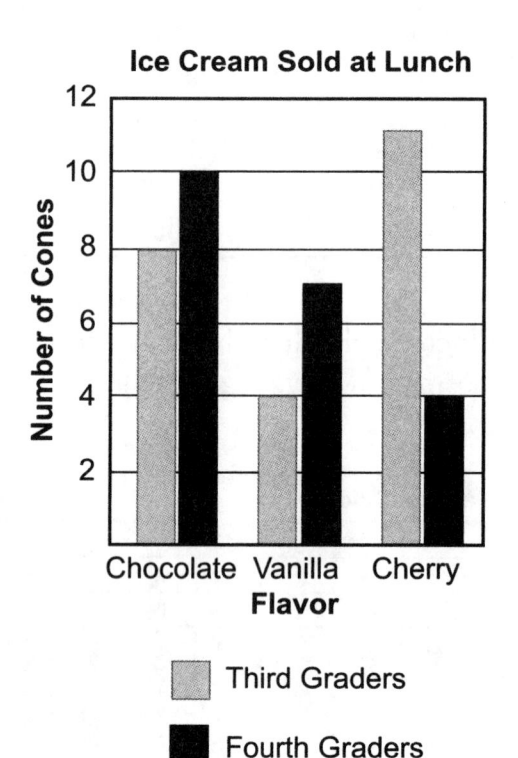

Ice Cream Sold at Lunch

Chocolate: Third Graders 8, Fourth Graders 10
Vanilla: Third Graders 4, Fourth Graders 7
Cherry: Third Graders 11, Fourth Graders 4

(3.1A; 3.1D; 3.1F)
1. How many third-grade students bought chocolate ice cream cones?

   A 8
   B 10
   C 18
   D 20

(3.1A; 3.1D; 3.1F)
2. Which is one way to find the total number of vanilla ice cream cones bought by third-grade and fourth-grade students?

   A 8 + 4 + 11
   B 7 − 4
   C 4 + 7
   D 11 − 7

(3.1A; 3.1D; 3.1F)
3. How many more cherry cones did third-grade students buy than fourth-grade students?

   A 6
   B 7
   C 8
   D 15

(3.1A; 3.1D; 3.1F)
4. What was the total number of cones sold to third-grade students?

   A 11
   B 21
   C 23
   D 25

Reporting Category 4
Data Analysis and Personal Financial Literacy

Exercise 10

3.8B: Solve one- and two-step problems using categorical data represented with a frequency table, dot plot, pictograph, or bar graph with scaled intervals (Supporting Standard)

Use the graph below to answer questions 1–5.

The graph shows the number of medals won by 3 swimming teams from 3 schools.

Medals Won by Swimming Teams

Oakwood School	☆ ☆ ☆ ☆ ☆ ☆ ☆ ☆
Martin School	☆ ☆ ☆ ☆
Fairview School	☆ ☆ ☆ ☆ ☆ ☆

☆ = 3 medals

(3.1A; 3.1D; 3.1F)
1. How many medals did the team from Fairview School win?

    A 12
    B 18
    C 25
    D 30

(3.1A; 3.1D; 3.1F)
2. How many more medals did the team from Fairview School win than the team from Martin School?

    A 12
    B 10
    C 6
    D 2

(3.1A; 3.1D; 3.1F)
3. How many medals did the team from Oakwood School win?

    A 24
    B 16
    C 12
    D 8

(3.1A; 3.1D; 3.1F)
4. How many medals did the teams from Fairview School and Martin School win in all?

    A 10
    B 20
    C 30
    D 50

(3.1A; 3.1D; 3.1F)
5. How many medals did all 3 swimming teams win in all?

    A 30
    B 36
    C 42
    D 54

Reporting Category 4
Data Analysis and Personal Financial Literacy

Exercise 11

3.8B: Solve one- and two-step problems using categorical data represented with a frequency table, dot plot, pictograph, or bar graph with scaled intervals (Supporting Standard)

Use the following information to answer questions 1 and 2.

The school nurse uses a frequency table to track the number of students that visit her office each week. The frequency table below shows the number of students in her office last week.

Student Visits to Nurse

Day	Tally
Monday	||||| ||
Tuesday	||||| |||||	
Wednesday	||||
Thursday	||||| ||||| |||
Friday	|||||

(3.1A; 3.1D; 3.1F)

1. What was the total number of students that went to the nurse's office last week?

   A 30
   B 35
   C 40
   D 45

(3.1A; 3.1D; 3.1F)

2. How many more students went to the nurse's office on Thursday than on Wednesday?

   A 4
   B 9
   C 13
   D 17

(3.1A; 3.1D; 3.1F; 3.1G)

3. Mr. Smith asked his students to name their favorite seasons. The results are shown below.

   Favorite Seasons

Season	Number of Votes
Spring	☁☁
Summer	☁☁☁
Fall	☁
Winter	◖

   If 12 students chose summer, how many students does the symbol ☁ represent?

   A 2
   B 4
   C 6
   D 8

(3.1A; 3.1D; 3.1F)

4. For two weeks in July, Annabelle kept track of the high temperature at her home. She recorded the information on the dot plot below.

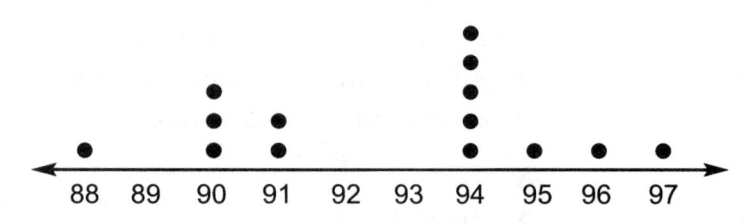

   Temperatures at Annabelle's House (°F)
   (88, 89, 90, 91, 92, 93, 94, 95, 96, 97)

   On how many more days was the high temperature 94 °F than 90 °F?

   A 2
   B 3
   C 5
   D 8

Reporting Category 4
Data Analysis and Personal Financial Literacy

Exercise 12

3.9: Apply mathematical process standards to manage one's financial resources effectively (3.9A, 3.9B, 3.9D, 3.9E)

(3.1A; 3.1E; 3.9A)

1. Jackson earns spending money by helping his mother pull weeds from her vegetable garden. The table below shows how much money he can earn.

Jackson's Earnings

Number of Hours	$ Earned
1	$0.50
2	$1.00
3	$1.50
4	$2.00
5	
6	$3.00

What number should fill the empty box in the table?

A $1.00
B $2.50
C $3.50
D $5.00

(3.1A; 3.1G; 3.9B)

2. On Monday, Green Grocery Store only received half of its weekly shipment of milk. During that week, what most likely happened to the price of milk at Green Grocery Store?

A Milk was free.
B The price increased.
C The price decreased.
D The price didn't change.

(3.1A; 3.9D)

3. Rosewood Elementary School is having a book fair in the library. Courtney wants to buy a book today but doesn't have any money with her. The librarian says Courtney can buy the book on credit. If Courtney buys the book on credit, who must pay for the book?

A No one
B Courtney
C The librarian
D Rosewood Elementary School

(3.1A; 3.9E)

4. Read the list of items below.

Benefits of _____ for College
• The family is prepared when it needs the money. • The money the family saves will earn interest. • The family won't have to borrow money when it is time for college.

Which word or phrase best completes the title of this list?

A Credit
B Interest
C A Savings Plan
D A Checking Account

Reporting Category 4
Data Analysis and Personal Financial Literacy

Exercise 13

3.9: Apply mathematical process standards to manage one's financial resources effectively (3.9A, 3.9B, 3.9D, 3.9E)

(3.1A; 3.1E; 3.1F; 3.9A)

1. Sasha earns spending money by helping her neighbors wash their cars. The table below shows how much money she can earn.

Sasha's Earnings

Number of Cars	$ Earned
1	$4.00
2	$8.00
3	$12.00
4	$16.00
5	
6	$24.00

What number should fill the empty box in the table?

A $15.00   C $20.00
B $18.00   D $28.00

(3.1A; 3.9E)

2. Read the list of items below.

Reasons to _____
• I will stay focused on my goal. • I will have enough money when I need it. • I won't need to borrow money when I need it.

Which word best completes the title of this list?

A Borrow   C Save
B Lend   D Spend

(3.1A; 3.1G; 3.9B)

3. Read the paragraph below.

> *The strawberry is a summer fruit. The best time to buy fresh strawberries is between June and August.*

In June, Janice went to the store to buy fresh strawberries. In December, she bought strawberries again. Which of the following did Janice most likely notice about the price of fresh strawberries?

A The price was the same all year long.

B Fresh strawberries were free in the winter.

C The price of fresh strawberries was lower in the winter than in the summer.

D The price of fresh strawberries was higher in the winter than in the summer.

(3.1A; 3.1G; 3.9D)

4. Mrs. Webber needed to replace her refrigerator. She didn't have enough money saved to pay for the refrigerator completely. Which of the following did Mrs. Webber most likely use to buy the refrigerator?

A Credit
B Interest
C Labor
D Receipt

Reporting Category 4
Data Analysis and Personal Financial Literacy

Exercise 14

3.9: Apply mathematical process standards to manage one's financial resources effectively (3.9A, 3.9B, 3.9D, 3.9E)

(3.1A; 3.1E; 3.1F; 3.9A)

1. Marisol earns spending money by helping her grandmother on the weekends. The table below shows how much money Marisol can earn for doing different jobs.

Marisol's Earnings

Job	Payment
collecting the mail	$0.25
taking out the recycling	$0.50
pulling weeds from the garden	$1.00
watering the indoor plants	$0.25

If Marisol does all of the jobs, how much can she earn in one week?

A $1.55
B $1.75
C $1.90
D $2.00

(3.1A; 3.9A)

2. Benjamin earns $3.00 every time he bathes the family dog. How many times does Benjamin have to wash the dog before he will earn $15.00?

A 4
B 5
C 6
D 7

(3.1A; 3.1G; 3.9B)

3. In August 2011, the temperature reached 100° in San Antonio for 12 days in a row. What most likely happened to the price of electricity for customers during that time?

A The price of electricity was the same as usual.
B The price of electricity was higher than usual.
C The price of electricity was lower than usual.
D Customers did not have to pay for electricity.

(3.1A; 3.9E)

4. Read the list of benefits below.

Benefits of _____

- It will help you make wise decisions.
- It will help you stay focused on your goals.
- It will help you prepare for an unexpected event.
- It will help you reach goals that are important to you.

Which word or phrase best completes the title of this list?

A Credit
B Interest
C A Savings Plan
D A Checking Account

Fraction Strips

1 whole												
$\frac{1}{2}$						$\frac{1}{2}$					
$\frac{1}{3}$				$\frac{1}{3}$				$\frac{1}{3}$			
$\frac{1}{4}$			$\frac{1}{4}$			$\frac{1}{4}$			$\frac{1}{4}$		
$\frac{1}{5}$				$\frac{1}{5}$		$\frac{1}{5}$			$\frac{1}{5}$		$\frac{1}{5}$	
$\frac{1}{6}$		$\frac{1}{6}$		$\frac{1}{6}$		$\frac{1}{6}$		$\frac{1}{6}$		$\frac{1}{6}$	
$\frac{1}{8}$	$\frac{1}{8}$	$\frac{1}{8}$	$\frac{1}{8}$	$\frac{1}{8}$	$\frac{1}{8}$	$\frac{1}{8}$	$\frac{1}{8}$			
$\frac{1}{10}$	$\frac{1}{10}$	$\frac{1}{10}$	$\frac{1}{10}$	$\frac{1}{10}$	$\frac{1}{10}$	$\frac{1}{10}$	$\frac{1}{10}$	$\frac{1}{10}$	$\frac{1}{10}$		
$\frac{1}{12}$	$\frac{1}{12}$	$\frac{1}{12}$	$\frac{1}{12}$	$\frac{1}{12}$	$\frac{1}{12}$	$\frac{1}{12}$	$\frac{1}{12}$	$\frac{1}{12}$	$\frac{1}{12}$	$\frac{1}{12}$	$\frac{1}{12}$